M6
SIGHTS
GUIDE

By Mike Jackson

Severnpix

Design: Lisa Griffiths

PLEASE NOTE: DRIVERS MUST NOT USE THIS BOOK WHILST AT THE WHEEL
PLEASE DEVOTE 100% CONCENTRATION TO SAFELY DRIVING ALONG THE MOTORWAY

ACKNOWLEDGMENTS

Our thanks to the hundreds of people who told us what went on where they lived or worked; and to librarians for swiftly and effectively directing us to the relevant local history sections of their shelves.

Thanks to John Elkington and Peter Sutton for proof-reading and good counsel, to Ben Jackson for chauffeuring, to Gil Jackson for logistics and to Peter Mitchelson for road-testing.

We are very grateful to Chris Burnley for his knowledge and guidance on all railway matters. Oh, yes, and to Lisa's husband, Ashley, for the Aston Villa entry, for which he accepts complete responsibility.

For having advised, supported and platformed us with our first endeavour, the M5 Sights Guide, many thanks to Anne-Marie and Stuart Phillips-Broadfield of Beacon Books, Malvern, Andi Klisuric of Waterstones, Worcester, and Marianne Holdsworth of Ottakar's, Bromsgrove.

Many thanks to everyone who encouraged us with our M5 Guide – the journalists who gave us excellent exposure and commentary, and the thousands of people who bought a copy.

THE M6 SIGHTS GUIDE

ISBN 0-9545402-1-2

First published by:
Severnpix
P.O. Box 468, Worcester WR6 5ZR
1st October 2004
www.severnpix.co.uk

Our special thanks to MG Rover, and Pat Gatsby and Nicola Ferrie in particular, for sponsoring our undertaking by providing us with an excellent new Rover 45 Club SE in which we could comfortably, safely and proudly undertake our field research.

They had seen how we had got 140,000 miles worth of motoring out of our old Rover 214 - not least in researching, road-testing, publicising and distributing our M5 Sights Guide - and saw fit to improve our image, quality of life and status on the road for this book.

We hope and trust they will continue to produce many fine cars from Longbridge in the decades ahead.

IMPORTANT NOTICE TO DRIVERS AND READERS

Drivers must not use this book whilst travelling. Additionally we recommend that passengers do not read the contents aloud whilst the vehicle is moving. Please devote 100% concentration to safely driving along the motorway.

Drivers must take sole responsibility for driving safely on the motorway and elsewhere. To the fullest extent permitted by law the authors and the publisher exclude their liability for loss or damage arising from any misuse of this publication.

INTRODUCTION

The Guide attempts to identify and describe every object of some significance that a passenger in a vehicle would easily be able to notice whilst travelling along the motorway.

Last year that was what our book about the M5 set out to achieve. Now I am applying the same principles to the M6.

Our first title arrived back in bulk from the printers on the 20th November 2003, and six months later we had sold almost all of the 6,000 print run – which is extremely small beer by the standards of popular literature, but I am assured is pretty good for a guide book.

If you bought a copy, thank you.

Essentially we got lots of publicity, triggering interest in the publication, not just along the M5 corridor but beyond. The ultimate accolade was Martin Townsend, the Editor of the Sunday Express, devoting his Easter Sunday column to our endeavour: "The success of Jackson's book has been reported with the combination of glee and incredulity normally reserved for the birth of lambs with two heads or the exploits of centenarian marathon-runners.

"Why would anyone want a book about miles of heavily-congested tarmac? The fact is the M5 book, with its earnest trivia about supermarkets and service stations, is irresistible to us because the British have a fascination for the quirky eccentricities of their own landscape – and for searching out the meanings of the buildings and monuments around them."

That is certainly what we did, and what I have tried to do again.

My route to the format for our Guides came from trying to design a book about the Malverns that combined geography with sights, whilst, in parallel, I was working on 'Antiques Roadshow' programme openings, packaging local history and pretty pictures for that week's location. Then it dawned on me that there were many more book shops along the motorway than around Malvern.

As I wandered the M5 corridor with my Ordnance Survey map, camera and notebook, I feared constantly that someone else had hit on the same idea and was in the midst of undertaking a similar task. It was with relief that I learned no other researcher had recently called on particular premises seeking data for their forthcoming title tackling the sights of the carriageway. My most anxious time was visiting the London Book Fair in the Spring of 2003 with a mock-up of some of our pages, expecting to see a glossy, finished version of something alarmingly like our embryonic guide sitting awaiting a massive publicity campaign backed by a major publisher.

Since going to press, I have discovered that I am merely queuing in a long line of topography-minded journalists following a well-trodden route.

Only recently I came across cartographer John Ogilby's 1675 illustrated road map of the coaching route from London to Aberystwyth. Same principle - show people what they can see on the way - beautifully executed, with a rolling parchment presentation of the course of the road showing major, mostly natural, features on either side.

Jeffrey Howarth of the National Trust had already drawn my attention to Paterson's Road Book of 1822 - unillustrated but using text layout to indicate geographic relationships - and The Rail Road Book of England of 1851 by E. Churton, using similar principles as Paterson.

The appearance of the motorcar in the 20th century unleashed lots of guide opportunities and options. Foremost, the AA Road Book of England and Wales was a formidable work especially through the 1930s, every road and town of any consequence getting some sort of entry, not necessarily enthusiastic: "Itinerary 413, Birmingham to Leicester via Nuneaton. The direct route, but with no noteworthy scenery. Mining about Nuneaton and Hinckley."

In 1955, just a few years before the first short stretches of motorway were laid, Christopher Trent gave us his

"Motorists Companion on the Highways of England" (published by George Newnes of The Strand, WC2) which brought photography into the frame: occasional black and white panels between long, meandering essays on the major arteries: "If Derby strikes the visitor as a town of contrasts, its shire is one of even greater and more arresting contrasts."

In 1993 Noel Whittall and Chris Oxlade set out to do for the M1 and A1 what Kristina Thimm and I later attempted to their west with their "What's that over there?" Whilst we were still refining our layout I ordered a copy of this potential format competitor from Malvern library and was frankly relieved when I saw their approach. They attempt to integrate illustrations with graphic design and text, but did not settle on a neat way of making the pages easily comprehensible and instead required a rather crude numbering system to connect the motorway layout with each entry.

Surrey-based map designer Dave Brooker e-mailed us after seeing our first wave publicity in the Mail on Sunday to advise us of his experiences of having produced a clever and neat presentation of the sights of the M25, "Scenes from a Motorway". It's a double-sided fold-out map for use on clockwise and anti-clockwise journeys as appropriate, with colour photographs of essential structures. He got plenty of publicity but couldn't persuade the motorway service areas to carry it.

Virgin Trains offer travellers a Windowgazer Guide. This is colourful and stylish, but again depends on an irritating numbering system to associate text and photographs with route positions. And like most of its predecessors, it heavily cherry-picks, pausing on the pretty, ignoring the ugly.

So the most significant thing that we did differently was be democratic about what's out there; not confine ourselves to the grand and distinctive, but include the ordinary, the functional, and establish a way of presenting them relentlessly along every page with the route lying elastically along the middle.

Kristina began our M5 book with attractive and effective line drawings of everything from churches to tower blocks, but we decided this approach was too time consuming and so changed to photography. I was taking pictures anyway to give her references to work from.

To fill our pages we have squeezed the real world left and right, up and down, compressing or expanding actuality to juxtapose the sights, which are supplemented by commentary on the places featured on the blue and brown motorway signs. And look out for a few personal recollections on the pages, reflecting my life in connection with the M6.

Most of the photographs were taken in the summer of 2004. In the winter more man-made structures may be visible than our pages indicate. Many of the trees pre-date the motorway, whilst others have been planted close to the hard shoulders to create a screen, which we have respected.

As the trees grow taller and commercial development continues, the scenery steadily changes, but Lisa Griffiths and I hope we have just about captured it and that it will have a validity for at least a few years. (Kristina Thimm has been unable to continue working with me on this project due to other commitments.)

Those familiar with the First Edition of the M5 book will know we anticipated considerable feed-back from individuals who had knowledge or views on our original entries. We were very surprised that so little was forthcoming. Even the press officers of the big plc companies did not attempt to bring

fresh perspectives to our attention. Did they not care, or fear we would mock their attempts at positive spin? Who knows. So again, rather than be definitive, we have endeavoured to provide curious, eclectic and sometimes amusing information about what we encountered along our way.

Upon completing my field researches, I sensed there is a bigger message than spotting interesting things from A to B. I journeyed northward to collect my data and pictures, and having reached Hadrian's Wall east of Carlisle, decided to carry on to the coast. Chance rather than plan took me to Whitehaven, once the third biggest port in England, where the Lowthers had fuelled their empire by getting the locals to hack coal from under the sea. Now on the promenade we find a 24 hour Tesco - a contemporary empire, to which many bow, currently looking to further extend its Whitehaven site, and hence suck yet more of the lifeblood out of the town centre. At the other end of the M6 the A14 now provides a trunk route from Felixstowe, Britain's biggest container port. And so I have acquired a notion of goods imported by sea to East Anglia and making it to the M6, then westward and upward until they come off the motorway and head out to Whitehaven to stock those supermarket shelves. Of course, in truth, most of the products will go through various logistics, warehousing and processing procedures before arriving at the beachhead of consumerism, but as a representation of our present day lifestyles, it's an analogy that one can constructively bear in mind. We have peppered our

world with supermarkets to satisfy our every appetite, and built routes across country so that lorries can deliver every conceivable foodstuff to our nearest out-of-town store. Yes, much of it has come from British farms, and only a proportion will have reached England by boat. Much more likely those dwarf bean packs and flowers have been flown into Britain. But you get it, don't you? Thousands of lorries shifting millions of products across the United Kingdom to indulge our every whim. We are consuming the planet, and destroying its atmosphere, its harmony, its life-giving environment.

Please let these thoughts inhabit your travels in parallel to our details of factories, farms, family histories and construction encountered along the route.

If you are using the M6 in the months ahead, then instead of simply participating in a miserable race along an anonymous channel of foliage, fencing and fly-overs, focused only on the distance to your exit, this Guide has the potential to forever enlighten your journey.

Mike Jackson   October 2004

234 MILES TO GO

If you are beginning your journey from north to south, then welcome to our pages. Check out our Principles and Practices at the back before proceeding.

Of course, some readers will start from the back and work forward and others will just hop on at junctions in the middle to head in either direction. Forgive us for the shortcomings in design and text that fail to accommodate all the odd points of arrival or departure. However, we are confident that every page can transform what might have been a motoring chore into an enriching experience.

DRAWDYKES CASTLE (N.O.)

Looking for lots of stones with which to build a distinctive dwelling? Well, weren't they lucky round here because they had Hadrian's wall to plunder. This pele tower is considered to mostly consist of Roman stonemasonry. It was the home of the Aglionby family through several centuries and has been re-built a couple of times, and was recently restored by Mike Milbourn.

One old guide book is dismissive of the edifice: "Though bearing the name, there is little about it to remind the spectator of those fortified structures with which the mind is accustomed to associate with the appellation of Castle." But it was good enough for General Leslie who master-minded the siege of Carlisle from here in 1645.

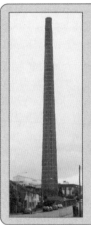

DIXON'S CHIMNEY

This took the smoke from the engine room of the Shaddon cotton mill. Originally 305 feet in 1836, it's been cut down to 270, but still makes for a heck of a sight, albeit it's also something of a liability. Carlisle Council felt obliged to buy the structure when no-one else wanted it after it became listed. They paid just £400, but have had to spend a fortune to ensure its stability.

TESCO (S.O.)

Open 24 hours to meet your every need. A quarter of Britons do the bulk of their food shopping at Tescos – of which there are nearly 800 branches, with more appearing all the time. As we travelled up and down the motorway we passed a considerable number of lorries in Tesco livery, and on several occasions also saw their Home Delivery vans scuttling about. We could fill this page with horror stories of how supermarkets treat their suppliers. Shame on so many of us for being willing participants in the various supermarkets' efforts to dominate our lifestyles and landscape.

BORDER MOTOR AUCTIONS

Part of the H&H (Harris and Hetherington) group, they hold sales every Tuesday and Friday, mostly achieving prices in the £200 to £3,000 range.

Lowest figure Graham Hall ever accepted for a car was £40, and at the top end, he once auctioned a Ferrari Testasomethingorother that had been seized by bailiffs, and which raised £25,000.

ST ELIZABETH'S, HARRABY

The plain square tower of this modern church in the middle of a big council estate enjoys a defining shape on the horizon. Outside it says: "Our mission is to become a family, where our love for Jesus inspires our worship, our care for one another, and our service in the community." Round the corner is a street of small well-supported shops of great variety, and here the Co-op has set up an all-needs emporium that will surely soon eliminate many of those individual premises and personal relationships between customers and staff.

CARLISLE-NEWCASTLE RAILWAY

This is one of Britain's oldest lines, dating from 1838. Amongst the services are boat trains to Stranraer for the ferry to Ireland and coal trains from Scotland heading for Tees-side steel works.

Note, be aware that where a railway crosses the carriageway, it gets a text reference on the side where the denotation of the line extends farther. Hence this refers to the northern of these two railway lines, and on the opposite page, where the lower, or southern, line extends outermost, we say something about that track.

See Principles and Practices on the inside of the back cover.

J44
8940
8914
J43
8879

BRUNSTOCK FARM HOUSE (S.O.)

The three-tier 1845 pink tower dominates this cluster of conversions that were the main and outbuildings of the farm – all very pretty and well-appointed, but not to the total satisfaction of the owners who are now seeking planning permission to move the main bathroom and to add an en suite.

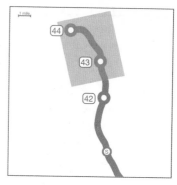

HADRIAN'S WALL

A couple of hundred metres north of Drawdykes Castle is the point where the motorway cuts through the line of the Wall. There's a long-term gypsy traveller camp immediately north of the road between Carlisle and Brampton on the west side of the carriageway, and indications of Hadrian's fortification can be found just beyond that. We went looking for it and discovered a long mound running east-west that defined it. We spoke to a local council worker who had never realised this was what he had been walking his dog past every evening.

RIVER EDEN

There are otters in this water, which meanders west into the eastern edge of Solway Firth, having risen a long way south in the Yorkshire Dales below Brough. The largest salmon caught in England came out of the Eden many years ago.

Note, rivers and canals are documented in blue italics, the extended waterline indicating the side of the carriageway on which we refer to that waterway.

See Principles and Practices on the inside of the back cover.

Carlisle

We don't attempt to replicate the stuff you can find in tourist bureaux. Instead we like the incongruous or obscure. In this fine town we had an excellent supper at Gianni's Pizzeria on Cecil Street, visited the 20-year old poky but personable Lonsdale Cinema that struggles against the might of newly-arrived Warner Village multi-screens, and saw lots of pretty girls in short skirts wandering in and out of pubs. A 12-year old gave birth to a baby boy last year.

Carlisle was where Britain's first green burial took place in 1993, using a biodegradable coffin and leaving no bulky headstone, so the location can later become a nature reserve or picnic area.

Now isn't that more memorable than gush about visiting the shopping malls and the museum?

Galashiels

Third top Google entry for this place is provided by the Scottish Campaign for Nuclear Disarmament who illustrate the effect of a major nuclear accident on Galashiels should such a thing happen at Chapelcross, Hunterston or Torness power stations, the Dounreay plant, or Faslane or Rosyth submarine docks.

Hawick

We old hacks from factual television reckon it takes a long time to put together a TV programme, so we were astounded when Hawick launched a three-day Video Making Competition in June 2004. Only broadcast news-makers should work at such speed was our view. Apparently the event was a great success with 20 entrants undertaking ambitious documentaries, promotional videos, dramas and even musicals. The winner was called 'A Road to Nowhere'.

Perhaps they should be given BBC4.

GET THE IDEA

Look, we're not going to tell you again. CHECK OUT THE PRINCIPLES AND PRACTICES PAGE AT THE BACK. We have created a weird elastic world, in contrast to Ordnance Survey planet where everything is strictly locked spatially to a measurable grid. Here everything is stretched and squeezed to work across our pages, up and down, left and right, east and west, north and south, and we are not even consistent on one part of any page. Good, eh!

SETTLE-CARLISLE RAILWAY

This is considered to be the most pleasing main-line railway journey. It was one of the last big routes to be constructed and required 13 tunnels and 21 viaducts, and lots of rough, tough workers who lived in crude conditions for several years in temporary camps across the Pennines. It came close to closure in the 1980s, but passionate enthusiasts lobbied for its maintenance and it survived. As well as passenger services (£16.80 for the return ride) it carries coal from Scotland to various Yorkshire and East Midlands power stations.

HARRABY RADIO STATION

Built in the late 1940s to relay television signals northward from London, it now provides line-of-sight microwave links for BT and other mobile phone operators - hence all the dishes on this 85 metre high steel structure. Underneath are offices which used to be part of the Ministry of Defence protected network communicating between government and military sites in the event of war.

THE CARLETON CLINIC

The bunch of buildings on the hill was originally the Garlands asylum, and is now part of the North Cumbria Mental Health and Learning Disabilities NHS Trust, employing 1,100 staff (including one of the most helpful and efficient PR people we have encountered on our travels, Deborah Prince) with a budget of £31 million. The clinic was opened by Frank Dobson when he was enjoying life as Secretary of State for Health in June 1999.

Hexham

50 people died in the market place in 1761 revolting against Pitt's attempts to swell the militia by means of random name-picking. They were shot by redcoats during the riot. This year, for the first time, it was decided to commemorate the event and stage a re-enactment - which shows that any half decent tourist board can dig up some old fact and turn it into a money-spinner.

J42

RIVER PETTERIL

The M6 runs parallel to much of this river, which rises just north of Penrith and drifts into the Eden in the middle of Carlisle. The River Eden and District Fisheries Association, REDFA, monitors and manages the fishing access in these parts. Cumbria has more fishing waters than any other English county.

LOWHURST COMPOUND

This is currently operated by Amey Mouchel for the Highways Agency, the executive agency of the Department of Transport responsible for operating, maintaining and improving the 5,130 miles of strategic roads in England that carry a third of all traffic and two thirds of all freight. Their aims: safe roads, reliable journeys, informed travellers.

RAVENSIDE

This Victorian pile has been the home of retired Carlisle baker James Johnson since he got married. The tower was added in the 1930s by the previous owner and provides a great view in all directions. The bakery business was taken over by Carrs of water biscuit fame.

The house has ten bedrooms and the lawns take 4 hours to cut.

THACKWOOD FARM

Margaret Wilson was told recently by Eden District Council to remove her National Farmers Union banner from her field because it advertises agriculture. She was incensed. Ironically she has distinctly mixed views about the NFU and has stopped subscribing because of their failure to support the grass roots. She thought the previous boss Ben Gill deserved his knighthood for being joined to the hip with Margaret Becket. During the foot and mouth crisis, whilst imprisoned on her farm, she erected a banner that read: "Blair fiddles while Cumbria burns." She is astounded that incompetent executives who failed to deal swiftly and sensibly with those problems are still in their jobs.

8817

8785

NEWLANDS FARM (N.O.)

Mr and Mrs Watson came down from New Galloway in Scotland to farm here in 1938. Mrs Watson agreed to come if she could have a new house, which was built for her, and then knocked down by the motorway contractors 30 years later, when it was decided it lay on the only route south. Another house was built for the couple, and their grandson now runs the place.

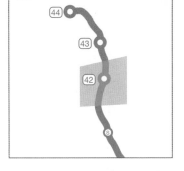

Newcastle

The Editor went to school here in his teenage years, and hated every minute of it. Gosforth Grammar School was a terrible place for a sickly, bespectacled stranger. Thankfully his evenings and weekends at Brunton Park were full of fun thanks to the Scouts and the youth club. And occasionally he got to go down town to see The Animals play upon their return from Top of the Pops. Local boys who made real good thanks to "The House of the Rising Sun".

Appleby

Here is one of the oldest and most distinguished schools in the country. It dates back to a foundation in 1286. At first a chantry priest provided lessons in the "Kyrke", but by the 15th century a separate Schoolhouse had been established. In Tudor times novice friars were taught Latin grammar. By 1700 it was the premier grammar school of the North, and still houses an exceptional library, built on the generous and expansive bequest of one of its 16th century headmasters, Reginald Bainbridge.

Every year the town attracts hundreds of gypsy travellers for family re-unions and horse trading. The people we met on the Corley northbound service area were on their way here.

CARLISLE-LANCASTER RAILWAY

This is the main line south, which motorway civil engineers had to work their way around along its route from here to beyond Penrith, hence it keeps crossing our carriageway above or below. So, rather than keep mentioning it, we've simply stuck a twist on the end of our track so you know which way it's coming or going. As well as passenger traffic it carries massive freight trains full of limestone out of the quarries at Shap.

FARM WORLD

Dairy and sheep farming are the biggest agricultural activities in Cumbria. Herds are more or less back to pre-foot and mouth levels: about half a million cattle and 2 million sheep. The warm, wet climate means excellent grass pasture which produces two or three crops of silage each summer. Some farmers are resentful of what they consider the National Farmers Union's accommodating attitude to the supermarkets. Margaret Wilson of Thackwood Farm has supported Farmers for Action-inspired pickets of Tescos for buying milk and meat abroad, not supporting local farmers, and charging so much for their products despite paying so little for them. "They walk all over us because we have a perishable commodity."

SUPERMARKET WORLD

Wouldn't you have thought that with their dominance of the market place Tescos could leave the fields for small companies to advertise their wares? But, no. North of here in the summer of 2004 Britain's biggest supermarket group positioned a banner to alert motorists heading north that a Tesco awaits them at Carlisle. Presumably as so many of us shop there, a good proportion of travellers may be suffering withdrawal symptoms.

In defence of Tesco, they do what they set out to do immensely well: that is, provide a vast range of foodstuffs and cleaning products at competitive prices under the one roof - which people want. It's the by-products of this achievement - not least the lorry miles and decline of High Street diversity - that worry us.

ROAD HAULAGE WORLD

The Road Haulage Association represents 10,000 members, who between them operate 100,000 vehicles. (This doesn't include white van man – of which there are around 3 million) The RHA provides advice on all sorts of issues, and presently has four main lobbying issues: fuel costs - European competitors can drive into the UK with vehicles full of far cheaper diesel; driver directives – the rules regarding patterns of work are very stringent and deny operators the flexibility which they say they need; congestion – yes, we've noticed that, and apparently it's the worst in Europe; and driver shortage: don't people want to do the job. Is the training too expensive, are the demands off-putting? The average age of a vocational HGV driver is 46.

8850

8833

8801

SOUTHWAITE NORTH

There's a tourist office here, opened by Willie Whitelaw in 1973, co-funded by Cumbria and the Scottish Tourist Board. Stupidest questions asked by visitors? For Staffer Andrew it was someone wanting to know if he needed a passport to get into Scotland and for Julie it was a woman wanting to know if she should take the M6 north or south to get to London.

SKELTON MAST

The 365 metre low frequency data transmitter pinpoints Skelton shortwave Radio Station built by the BBC in 1943 to send World Service signals to Europe. There is a forest of shorter towers at the site which bounce a dozen foreign language services to parts of Europe, the Middle East, North Africa and Central America.

KITTY HOUSE

Harris tenant Stan Threlkeld began his working life as a shepherd, then took up the accordian and played in a band. Then he ran a haulage business taking whisky from Scotland to Felixstowe. Now he drives round in a Triumph Vitesse previously owned by Robbie Coltrane, and he makes model aircraft and petrol-driven toy jeeps for kids.

HALLRIGG FARM

Ian Graham is a tenant of the Harris family (biggest landowners without a title who made their money from iron ore in West Cumbria and then took over the enormous Blackenbrook estate in the 1950s). Ian's an Eden District Councillor struggling to provide low cost affordable homes for young couples in the face of government quotas that severely limit new builds in the area.

LOW STREET FARM

Farmer Philip Clearkin remembers the motorway contractors dynamiting his trees to get them out of the ground easily, before they burnt them. His cows have to wade through a stream to get to the other side of the motorway. After heavy rain the water is black with muck from the carriageway. He went down the M6 once to visit the Royal Show and took a wrong junction which led him into Birmingham where he saw black people for the first time.

SADDLEBACK

On a clear day you can see the three peaks of Saddleback. From south to north they are Knowe Crags at 804 metres above sea level, Hallsfell Top at 868, and Tarn Crags at 845. Way beyond them is Skiddaw at 931. If you're going to explore, stop at the excellent Upfront Gallery and vegetarian coffee shop on the way at Unthank on the B5305.

CLOUGH HEAD

According to Will Robinson and Jim Davis of the Penrith Outdoor Centre shop, the hill that drops northward in a steady curve into a valley is Clough Head at 726 metres above sea level. The valley is that of the River Glenderamackin, which flows off Saddleback then south and west towards Keswick and Derwent Water.

Wigton

According to Bulmer's Directory of Cumberland of 1901, Wigton was a small but neat and well-built market town, occupying a pleasant situation on the right bank of the Wiza, 11 miles S.W. by W from Carlisle, 21 miles N.W. by W from Penrith, 15 miles N.N.E. from Cockermouth and 306 miles N.N.W. from London. "Red freestone is abundant, and is quarried at several places, but neither coal nor limestone has been met with."

3

8688

8656

J41

SOUTHWAITE SOUTH

Perhaps not the most impressive motorway service area frontage on the M6. However the Fresh Express restaurant does lots of leaflets telling us how and what to eat for health, ranging from our needs for calcium (stops bones disintegrating), through juice properties, to the value of dark fruits and vegetables (from warmer countries); and why prices sometimes seem so high.

A GAP ALREADY?

What - only a couple of pages in, and there's a space where the Editor reckons there's nothing worth seeing? Don't panic. This happens a few times along the route. Just patches where there's not much definitive. Altogether less than 20 miles out of the 234.

LAMBS TO THE SLAUGHTER

Swaledale twin lambs can be born as early as February, Herdwick single black lambs as late as June. Ewes manage about 8 years of breeding. 70% of the wool is exported for carpets, and quite a lot of the meat goes to Europe. For a cuddly woolly version of the story visit the Sheep and Wool Centre at Cockermouth. Good shop, café and toilets.

A TRIP TO THE SEASIDE

After weeks of hugging the M6, what a pleasant change it would make to visit the coast – all in the cause of research, of course. After having tracked down Hadrian's Wall at dusk, I decided to head for Maryport, which sounds nice. A long, dark drive through heavy rain eventually brought me to a bleak Dickensian grid of grim buildings, no pretty guest house in sight. So onward to Workington, hoping it would not be as bad as it sounds. I passed the enormous, scary Voridian polymer plant and in the dark could see no accommodation. So to Whitehaven, about which I feared the worst having read about the Lowther coal mines. Suddenly ahead a Travel Inn logo, and for the first time this icon of uniformity lifted my spirits. But there was no room at the inn and they forwarded me to a weird, converted school doing a roaring trade in wedding receptions in a utilitarian mining town inland where I spent a utilitarian night. The tourist board gives the place four crowns. Mm...

At dawn I headed into Whitehaven and had a satisfactory breakfast at a decent café on Lowther Street and enjoyed a walk along the jetty. I retraced my journey through Workington and Maryport and am sorry to report they seemed not that much better on a sunny morning. Many of the houses (changing hands for less than £50,000) are distinctly fundamental. Frontages not long enough to take the small saloon car often parked outside; one bedroom window above, sometimes with a satellite dish alongside. Barely adequate accommodation for mine workers and merchant seamen whose offspring can now enjoy the riches of the supermarkets dominating the ring road or the promenade 24 hours a day.

POT 34

On the site of Plumpton railway yard, Kevin Roper and Paul Thomas make concrete statues for gardens. Kevin trained in ceramics, but they can't get a three-phase power supply to the site so they concentrate on specialised concrete fountains, benches and figures ranging in price from £5 to £2,000, all much cheaper here than at garden centres.

DENTON COTTAGES (S.O.)

Serious joinery work going on here, involving welding metal beams. There's a sweet little bunch of barn conversions down the hill, and on the horizon the sun occasionally shines on the Civil Aviation radar sphere that sits atop Great Dun Fell about five miles north of Appleby.

MILESTONE HOUSE

Foremost of a group of small businesses occupying the land beside this house is Richard Nelles's tractor and machinery firm, supplying and servicing Ford, Massey Ferguson and Renault vehicles, and acting as agents for Hyundai fork lift trucks. Most of his customers are in Cumbria, but inexplicably there's a bloke in Liskeard in Cornwall who keeps ordering tractors from him through an ad. in Farmers Weekly. Not that he's complaining.

8672

Keswick

The Editor's memories of the town stem from making the opening to the Antiques Roadshow's visit, one of the last presented by Hugh Scully. It's a big responsibility deciding what to put in a programme seen by 10 million people all over the world as well as by the locals. What to include, what to leave out, where to point the camera? It focused on Robert Southey and Derwent pencils and completely ignored the crazy car museum which is great fun.

PRIME SUSPECT

"Many of you will be familiar with television portrayals of forensic science. Although glamourised, they give a reasonably accurate insight," according to the nearby Newton Rigg College (The University of Central Lancashire's Cumbria Campus). They are advertising a BTEC Diploma in the subject to equip you with the skills to enter employment as a volume crime scene examiner or fingerprint development technician.

Penrith

We like the look and feel of this town. It seems sturdy and sensible, perhaps best exemplified by the George Hotel, which has a timeless market town quality. There are lots of individual, old shop fronts, a delight to the eye after so many chain store facades. The first class tourist office does a terrific Millennium Trail folder full of guides to the treasures of the town for a mere 50 pence.

ALBA PROTEINS

You love your chicken breasts and legs. And some are hooked on nuggets. But what happens to the rest of every bird? Well, after the white bits have been sliced off, the remains come here for rendering. They have a category 3 poultry licence to process animal by-products not intended for human consumption. Yes, most of the rest of that chicken becomes pet food.

8608

Workington

205 Harrington Road is a not untypical estate agent's offering: "The accommodation comprises: Lounge: 12' x 11'; Dining kitchen: 11' x 8'; Bathroom: 7' x 5'; First floor: Bedroom 1: 11' x 10'; Bedroom 2: 11' x 8'; To the rear: concreted yard. £43,500."

BOWMANS BARN

This was built to accommodate horses and carriages, because from here the Bowman brothers run their successful horse-driving sport. 3-day dressage and marathon events determine who's best at walking, trotting and obstacles. George is way out in front having been National Champion 17 times. Robert's returned to the reins, recently inspired by driving horses and carriages for his son's wedding.

AIR AMBULANCE

The Bowmans's horses are unbothered by the motorway and railway, and even jet aircraft that pass overhead, so the brothers are not phased by plans to establish an air ambulance base around here.

ATKINSON

New offices for this small local building firm who have been doing renovations, new builds, bathroom improvements and barn conversions for 20 years across a 30 mile radius.

DOMINOS

This is a dough ball commissionary. A what? They make the fresh balls of dough that go on to become pizza bases for 73 Domino outlets in this part of the world. Well, we're talking all the way from Aberdeen to Nottingham. (2 other commissionairies deal with the other 240 UK outlets). The Penrith team of 34 also distribute the various toppings and tools that make a pizza a Domino, like aprons, cutters, boxes, delivery bags and hand wash.

COUNTY MOTORS

The Sherrard family have been selling cars in Cumbria since 1947. They began by putting Standard models next to their petrol pumps in Carlisle, then opened a garage in Penrith offering Triumphs in the 1950s.
Word of mouth and repeat business are the essentials says Mike Sherrard. Penrith's a homespun sort of town that does not need a hard sell. The staff are homely and friendly, and the customers keep coming back.

BOCM PAULS

This 70,000 tonnes per annum plant (small by the firm's standards) is one of only two doing organic cattle feed as well as the usual stuff. No chemicals go into the crops that become the feed, which makes them more expensive to produce. There's a good market for the end product – food for cows that will be slaughtered as organic beef, but they can't get enough non-chemically treated raw materials, especially beans and peas.

ALTHAMS

The Thomas Altham ironmongery business started in Penrith's Boroughgate back in 1844. Their old premises are now a wine bar, which the boss, Edwin Atkinson, reckons is probably an easier way to make money. Althams are proud of their product range that they say is far more extensive than the likes of Travis Perkins.

NORTH WEST DEVELOPMENT AGENCY

These were the offices of the Rural Development Commission, which was absorbed into the Agency last year. The Regional Development Agency has a budget of £345 million to "directly influence £1.2 billion of economically focused expenditure." The Business Investment Scheme will deliver £70 million of seed and venture capital investment to small to medium businesses from European Structural Funds.

Rheged

So what's going on here? The people behind Westmorland Services saw a gap in the market for an all-weather attraction. They've pulled together a mix of Cumbrian legend, achievements, talent and craft skills, and provided a pleasing environment in which to platform and celebrate flavours of the culture - with a big-screen cinema and climbing artefacts. Scariest rock world story we heard - the guy who got his arm wedged in a crevice and so had to hack it off.

LONSDALE COUNTRY

Around here we mere motorists are driving through some of the massive tracts of land that belong to the Lowther family, who date back to Viking times, when they managed to plunder most of this region. Later they got behind William of Orange who formally handed over most of Westmorland and Cumberland to them. A string of generations then indulged in excessive hunting, shooting and fishing, and when coal was discovered at Whitehaven, their indulgences really took off. Hugh Lowther (1857-1944) inherited the title the Earl of Lonsdale from his brother and went round killing animals and birds, riding horses, betting, boxing and partying across the globe, mixing it with Royalty, Lily Langtry and the German Kaiser. This ultimate hooray Henry got to be a government minister, Chief Steward of the Jockey Club, President of the AA and boss of Bertram Mills Circus. His whole life was a circus, as respectfully documented in Douglas Sutherland's fascinating book, The Yellow Earl. On property they have given up, the family ("very nice people") sometimes still own rights to any minerals that might one day be found below ground.

VIADUCT OVER LOWTHER

The River Lowther springs from the Shap Fells and helps form Wet Steddale reservoir before winding north to feed into the Eamont south east of Penrith.

Up at Plumpton (where Pot 34 are based) back in 1885 a police constable was shot dead by one of three criminals who had robbed a house near Carlisle and were attempting to make their getaway along the line.

LOW MOOR FARM

Following foot and mouth, Anthony Errington re-stocked with German red and white cattle, dual-purpose animals that can provide good milk and good beef.

We listened carefully to his explanations of the mechanics and timescale of cattle reproduction and lifespan and hope we got the hang of it. If a cow produces milk and calves she'll live for six years. Male animals will normally be slaughtered by 15 months.

BT PREMISES, HACKTHORPE

This houses the automatic telephone exchange which serves 800 customers in the area. Behind the village of Hackthorpe is the village of Lowther, which the Earls had moved from its original site as it was spoiling the approach to their castle. (Sorry, we do keep going on about those Lowthers).

TRAVELLING LIGHT (S.O.)

This warehouse, only the top of which you can see from the carriageway if you are in a normal saloon car, services the 9 shops and mail orders for a clothing company based in Workington set up three years ago by Freddy and Susie Markham – the UK's leading retailer and manufacturer of hot weather travel clothing – all designed and made in Cumbria.

North West Lakes

These are (east to west) Haweswater and Ullswater, separated by Bampton and Martindale Commons, then, to the west of Helvellyn, Thirlmere. The Westmorland Gazette recently reported that the Lake District has had its best ever year for tourism with 15 million visitors spending £1 billion in the region. They do a hell of a hard sell on Wordsworth: "The Adventurer, Lover, Rebel; England's Finest Poet."

Eden Valley

The Council employs a parking tsar, David Robinson, who issues newsletters updating motorists to new schemes that promote positive parking. Nationally over 2 million parking tickets are issued by councils across the land. Eden aims to move towards Decriminalised Parking Enforcement.

ENVIRONMENT AGENCY (S.O.)

Alas their good intentions are not reflected in paper generation. After a degree of reluctance to hand over any information at all, they gave us documents weighing 1.3 kilograms to peruse. They are very proud of their environmentally-friendly building that houses the Nuclear Regulation Group responsible for monitoring Sellafield.

RIVER EAMONT

This flows out of Ullswater and heads east to the Eden, which meanders north towards Carlisle. It provides trout fishing if you know what you're doing: "The best flies are small and lightly dressed. Early in the year spiders are generally best (Olive Woodcocks and heavy nymphs) and from mid-May onwards, small dry flies can be introduced (Grey Dusters)."

CLIFTON TOWER (S.O.)

This is all that remains of Clifton Hall, once occupied by the Wybergh family who ran into debt in the 17th century and so were forced to sell most of their land to Sir John Lowther. They hung on to the Hall and improved it in the 18th century, but then sold it to the Lowthers in the 19th century. Most of it was demolished before the Lowthers gave it to the Department of the Environment in 1973, who in turn handed it over to English Heritage.

WHITEHOUSE STABLES

John and Mary Robinson live in the three-level building, one of a cluster converted from stables that used to belong to the Lowthers. The couple are fearful that plans are afoot to build a motorway service area on the land. Watch that space. Behind the stables is the Whitehouse guest house, where we spent a very comfortable night.

BAINBRIDGE GATE

This building was a billet for the English army during the Battle of Clifton Moor of 1745, a skirmish with the Scots a year before Culloden. It's owned by the Lowther family, constituting a tiny element of one of the 20-odd businesses registered at the Lowther Castle estate office, such as Lake District Homes Ltd and Garden of Eden in Cumbria Ltd.

SELDOM ASKED QUESTION

Why is the AA so yellow? The 5th Earl of Lonsdale – never backward in coming forward – used to ride round town in a horse-drawn coach done up in the family's bright yellow insignia. When cars came in, the horse-loving Lord was rightly suspicious of the machine's reliability, so, if he were to use one, he'd have a stand-by running along behind, for if and when the first broke down. Both vehicles were painted in his house-style yellow. Somehow Hugh Lowther got to be President of the AA. The concept of the stand-by car seemed most appropriate for the early Automobile Association and so they went with the Earl's colour scheme for their vehicles.

EMPEROR'S LODGE

Hugh Lowther rode lots of up-market social horses, befriending both the Prince of Wales (later Edward VII) and Kaiser Wilhelm, the German Emperor, before the First World War. As a bit of a surprise for the visiting Kaiser, Hugh had these gatehouses knocked up as a novel route to Lowther Castle. Who knows how they went down, but Hugh worked vigorously during the war to encourage lots of Brits to head for the front. We knew nothing of Lowthers or Lonsdales until we investigated these castellations amongst trees and discovered a route across parkland past the now crumbling remains of the once 100 bedroom Lowther Castle. The estate office manager kindly showed us a coloured map of how the now merely 77,000 acre estate is deployed amongst farmers and other tenants.

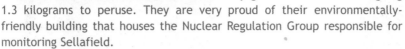

LOOK WEST

The distinctive triangular peak occasionally visible from here is Kidsty Pike at the southern end of High Raise, which reaches 208 metres above sea level.

HANSON QUARRY

They extract a million tonnes of limestone a year, half of which goes down to Corus by rail a few miles south, the rest by rail to Redcar for steel manufacture, or for aggregates for road building, or for farmers' fertiliser or for the underlay material in Scottish carpets.

CORUS SHAPFELL

These kilns burn off impurities of quarried limestone to provide 60% (8,400 tonne) of Corus's weekly need of high grade metallurgical lime for steelmaking. At between 1,000 and 1,200 degrees centigrade, the calcium carbonate in the limestone is calcined, with carbon dioxide being driven off as a gas and calcium oxide remaining. The plant takes pride in its environmental record, and who are we to gripe as all our cars have been created from bits that were put together thanks to this process.

WESTMORLAND NORTH SERVICES

As well as an award-winning service area, they have a hotel and a caravan park here. We enjoyed a comfortable night in the hotel, which was opened by David Bellamy in 1997. It's stylish and distinctive, and "lots of lords and ladies have stayed here". The concrete tower as you approach the slip road holds a water tank for servicing the sewage from the site.

PROPOSED WHINASH WINDFARM

In July 2004 hundreds of people marched across Whinash Ridge to the west in protest over plans to erect a massive wind farm across the top. The intention is to erect 27 machines each 115 metres high with a blade diameter greater than the wingspan of a jumbo jet. Melvyn Bragg and Alan Titchmarsh are amongst the celebrities against it. They say an unspoilt wilderness will be desecrated, ruining the gateway to the Lake District and the tourism economy. In August 2004 John Prescott announced a relaxation of planning permission rules for wind farms inside national parks.

8480

8472

8464

8440

J39

3.5

8336

J38

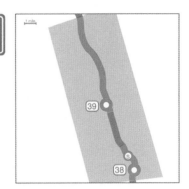

North Pennines

One of the curious repercussions of the development of tourism services by councils is that there is a wish to concentrate all resources and publicity into the relevant geographic area and completely ignore what's beyond. This is the case with the North Pennines to the east of Cumbria, almost invisible as regards locally available literature.

Scotch Corner

Seldom does a week go by on Radio Two in the afternoons without Sally 'Traffic' Boazman mentioning this key junction on the A1M south of Darlington in connection with an accident and hold-up in that vicinity. The A66 is the weather-challenged trunk road crossing the Pennines from there to the M6 at Junction 40 and via the A685 from Tebay to Brough.

RECOGNISE THAT SHEEP?

Do they all look the same? Well, not to other sheep. The Babraham Institute in Cambridge recently published a scientific study about the fact that sheep experience measurable signs of happiness when they are shown photographs of their relatives and friends. Looking at such pictures can reduce their separation anxiety. The animals can remember up to 50 individual sheep faces, even in profile, and up to a dozen familiar human faces.

Shap

The English railway network reaches its highest point near here at 900 feet (275 metres). Last winter a wagon loaded with old rails broke free at Stout Green depot and rolled down the track southward for three miles towards Tebay, killing four workers on the line before dawn.

SHAP SUMMIT

Many a traveller has come unstuck trying to get across here, particularly in bad weather, of which there's plenty. The rail route has destroyed locomotives and the old A6 saw off a number of lorry drivers frozen to death in or around their cabs, but Highways Agency snow ploughs and gritters have kept a motorway route across the top (1,036 feet above sea level) open most of the time. The separated carriageways help to make the thoroughfare usable in all circumstances.

MILES

WESTMORLAND SOUTH SERVICES

On their paper napkins they tell us: "It is the only Motorway Service Area to be built and run by local people. Much of the food we offer is produced and prepared in Cumbria. The buildings reflect the style of Cumbrian houses and farmsteads. Other services on the motorway are part of large corporate organisations who pride themselves on their uniform service throughout the country."

The Farm Shop was opened by Prince Charles in February 2004.

BYBECK FARM (N.O.)

Heather Roberts breeds semi-wild fell ponies from here. The mares have their foals in May and spend July and August with the stallion. Then in September the adult mares are allowed back up on to Howgill Fells to forage, the young foals staying at Bybeck for their first winter. And they've all got names.

J38 TRUCKSTOP

The Autogas sign above the petrol station indicates the site of this lorry drivers' rest and recreation facility operated by Westmorland Services here for the last 20 years.

LOOKING SOUTH

Those are Tebay Fells ahead (highest point: Knott, 391 metres). You're going to veer right (west) into the Lune Valley.

Tebay

This was once a key depot of the Lancaster-Carlisle railway line, part of the London North Western Railway which, for a number of years before the First World War, was Britain's biggest public company, when it had over 3,000 locomotives and over 80,000 carriages or wagons and an equal number of employees. Its income in 1911 was £16 million.

RIVER LUNE

Divers are allowed by the Tourist Board to jump... sorry... dive into the river at Devil's Bridge on the A65 at Kirkby Lonsdale between November and January each year. They report the water as reddish brown, 7 degree centigrade with visibility between 0.5 and 1 metre. And the current damn fast. "We spent a good hour in there though."

FOOT AND MOUTH

A Public Inquiry examined the impact of the disease across Cumbria (which used to be Cumberland and Westmorland), one of the largest and most sparsely populated Counties of England. Foot and Mouth reduced the economy of the county by 4% compared with 0.2% for the UK as a whole.

CIVIC TRUST AWARD

On the A685 above us to the west is a pull-in area from which motorists can admire the motorway below. And in case they didn't realise they were meant to admire it, there's a big plaque placed on the end of the car park by the Civic Trust in 1971, acknowledging their Award "for an outstanding contribution to the appearance of the Westmorland landscape relating to the 36 miles of motorway between the Lancaster and Penrith by-passes. Designed by Scott Wilson Kirkpatrick and Partners, Consulting Engineers; Bridges: Ansell and Bailey; Contractors: W & C French, John Laing, Christiani Shand and Tarmac."

ROCK OUTCROPS (S.O.)

Heading south, to your right (west), you can see a line of very distinctive crags on the horizon on sunny days. They are Little Coum and (to the left) Great Coum, part of Grayrigg Pike, which reaches 494 metres above sea level.

KENDAL-PENRITH RAILWAY

This is the main line from Lancaster to Carlisle, which crosses over or under the M6 half-a-dozen times along the Lune Valley and beyond northward; so rather than keep mentioning it, from here upward, we've just put a twist on the end of our track so you know which way it's coming and going. Some of the fastest ever steam train journeys have been recorded on the downhill stretches either side of Shap summit.

Sedbergh

Why do we go for the curious rather than rely on the tourist literature? Because so much of the latter has a horrible, bland, generic quality, like this place's leaflet: "An historic market town", "dating from Roman times", " a fine Norman church", "stroll along the banks of the meandering river", "Farfield Mill is now an arts and crafts heritage centre." Doubtless lovely and well worth a visit, it's 5 miles east of Junction 37.

LAMBRIGG PARK FARM

The Potter family lost 40 acres with the arrival of the M6 here. There used to be a small lake just to the south that was slowly but surely filled in with huge rocks cut by the contractors from the west side of the Lune Valley to the north. Massive dumper trucks carried the stone past the front of the farmhouse, turning the ground into something like slurry in the process, which made it impossible to drive the tractor. The farmhouse was once a busy inn, lying on the main droving route from Scotland.

LAMBRIGG WIND FARM

This was developed by National Wind Power Limited, and constructed by David McLean, with electrics by Agrilek and turbines by Bonus Energy. Over the last few years the north west has produced 37% of the UK's wind-generated electricity. Lambrigg can generate enough power to meet the needs of 4,000 homes - assuming the wind's blowing, of course!

UNIPEN

The big silver shed sitting on the site of the old railway depot is the base for a company which has the contract to service the massive underground ethylene pipeline that lies underneath and carries natural gas south from Grangemouth to the Wirral.

JUNCTION HOTEL

This was once a popular stopping place for visitors to the area on pleasure or business, but now it's been transformed into private homes, one of which is occupied by formidable anti-wind turbine campaigner Doctor Eve Bomino, who doesn't oppose alternative energy sources in principle, but doesn't want a line of turbines spoiling the view from her windows.

Brough

A 1777 County History considered "The Church at Brough is a pretty large handfome ancient building. The fteeple is not fo old, having been built about the year 1513, under the direction of Thomas Blenkinfop. There are in it four excellent bells, by much the largeft in the county, except for the great bell at Kirkby Thore."

BLEASE FELL

A tight squeeze above the Lune round the base of the 474 metre Blease Fell to the east. See that heart-shaped woodland on the hillside. Best story we have heard is that a pilot crashed and died there and that his mourning fiancé wanted a memorial and the council wouldn't let her put anything permanent but said she could plant a tree, so she put all those ones in the ground.

BECK FOOT VIADUCT

This identifies an old line that ran south to Sedburgh, Kirkby Lonsdale and beyond, a victim of the Beeching cuts. In 1963 Richard Beeching recommended that the Conservative Government close 266 passenger services, 2,363 stations and 8,500 miles of track.

MOORCOCK HALL

Brian Oversby has been a tenant here since 1958. His landlord bought the place for £200 during a day-long auction of 40 farms in the area being sold off from the Underley estate. Brian worked as a lorry driver for the construction of the motorway which was three and a half years in the making in these parts. It took eight months to hack out a flat segment from the side of the Grayrigg Pike below the line of the A685 to form the base of the M6 up towards Tebay.

KILLINGTON LAKE SERVICES

This Roadchef site has the best view, looking across Killington Reservoir, dug out to provide a source of water for the Lancaster Canal. In the building is a Wishing Well operated by the local Rotary Club for St John's Hospice. "Life is a journey, travel it well." Last year this plastic bin padlocked to the wall raised £1,000. There's a tourist office which we hung round in for five minutes hoping the woman behind the counter would come off the phone from criticising some badly-dressed colleague to a friend, but she didn't. Note, this may be the last place to stock up on Kendal Mint Cake before heading south. We bought six and consumed three before we reached the Midlands.

HILL FARM (N.O.)

Alan Wilson knows weather like most of us can only imagine – but worse. This place lies at a point on the hills highly vulnerable to cross winds. He's seen cast iron spouts from the side of the house blow over the top and into the fields. And once a 300 gallon capacity steel diesel tank parked on his drive was blown right up to the door, blocking him in.

Barrow

This place is fascinating for lovers of maritime heritage. It's got a great museum full of fabulous models of ships built in the docks. Driving around the docks themselves one is sobered by the sight of the tenement-like apartment buildings that housed the workers. And it's possible to catch sight of a Trident submarine under maintenance.

Kendal

Home of the Mint Cake. Who needs to know more? Okay, a 71 year old Kendal plumber was fined £60 for speeding when caught on camera. He later made a V-sign at the camera, which captured the gesture, and so he then got fined £100 for not being in control of his vehicle.

PRESTON PATRICK CHURCH

The vicar based here was "struck off" for apparently kissing too passionately a parishioner from the neighbouring Crosscake benefice. According to the lady weeding the war memorial, the old vicar was a friendly man who delivered nice sermons and was exceptionally good at funerals. The Church Commissioners, after consultations with the Bishop of Carlisle, have now allocated this church to the Kirkby Lonsdale Ministry and given Crosscake their own new vicar.

SHELL

One of the world's biggest petroleum companies saw its prestige run seriously downhill after it emerged that senior executives had been misrepresenting reserves. Despite the shame and share devaluation the Anglo-Dutch management saw fit to give their ousted head of exploration and production Walter van de Vijver a £2.5 million pay-off; far more than the disgraced former chairman Sir Philip Watts who had to make do with £1 million plus an annual pension of over £500,000. Meanwhile Chairman Ron Oxburgh recently admitted that climate change makes him "really very worried for the planet."

LANCASTER CANAL

How do you keep a canal full of water up here? By creating a reservoir at Killington that will hold 766 million gallons and supply 17 million gallons a day. That was done back in 1819. The canal was seriously hit by the opening of the Lancaster-Preston railway in 1840, and so in 1842 obtained a lease for the railway for an annual rent of £13,300. Both were later sold to the LNWR.

GRAVEL LORRIES

There's a big active quarry just south of Holme Park Farm from which wagons full of gravel roar up towards Junction 36 along the lane in front of Farleton hamlet. There's no speed limit, and seemingly no sense of caution by the drivers from Saunders, Thursbys, Bartons, Ollertons, James Booths and Robinsons. One farmer told us he lives in fear of trying to cross his cattle over the lane, where one of his tractors was written off recently, the driver suffering broken bones. We were viciously tail-gated by a ruthless Robinsons's driver.

A DOG'S LIFE

At farms on our journeys we encountered lots of dogs on chains and some in small cages, and in one instance we contacted the RSPCA, who told us they'd investigate. Nothing to compare with the Gregson's home in Silverdale where 244 dogs were rescued from squalid conditions by the RSPCA last year.

Please note, they like a postcode before they investigate; grid references if possible.

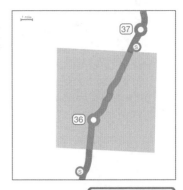

Christopher Trent, in his 1955 (yes, pre-motorway) Motorists Companion on the Highways of England describes the journey north from Carnforth towards Carlisle by leaving the A6 and heading for Windermere: "This is a real mountain road in miniature with many a thrilling view of abrupt rock faces and towering peaks. It is often said that a main road never does full justice to the intimate and elusive beauty of the English scene. In spring and autumn it is little used and stands out in the memory as a road of special distinction."

Skipton

Development executives for Disneyland might wince if they visit the castle here for inspiration, because it offers so much and yet none of it is made from fibre-glass. It's the real thing with battles and sieges to its name and orders from Cromwell to remove its roof. But in 1655 Lady Anne Clifford managed to get the roof back on (we don't know how) and since then the place has flourished. It's a charming mix of unspoilt medieval remnants and timeless, tasteful tearooms.

WHO NEEDS LANDSCAPES?

Tucked into a temporary gallery in a 16th century stone building alongside the motorway we discovered an exhibition of the abstract three-dimension work of Barrow boy John Hewitt keen to contrast with the "Sunday water-colourists". He uses MDF to stretch and shape canvas to capture his recollections of travelling through the landscape as a child in a car. They looked great. Check them out at www.abstractacrylicart.co.uk.

ATKINSON GARAGE

This place serviced the A65 Lancaster – Kendal road long before the motorway came along. They've been serving Shell for 35 years. Others brands before that. Long-time motor engineer Tony Westbury told us the difference the motorway made was that thieves could now get easy access. Villains from Glasgow and Liverpool try to steal vehicles from his yard. He has even had to rescue drug-dealers in hired cars broken down on the motorway. He was busy effecting a repair to a tear in the side of a caravan with strips of sticky Duck Tape, for which he would be charging £40 an hour.

FARLETON FELL

The National Trust recently re-instated an old dry stone wall across the top of the fell, and have been toying with putting cattle to graze up there.

HOLME PARK FARM

Horribly vulnerable to the gravel lorries roaring past is Andrew Threlkeld aboard his small four-wheel all-terrain vehicle. We caught him coming back on to his neatly-maintained yard to collect a plastic sack of chemicals. He has 200 milking cows producing 4,500 litres a day for the Wiseman milk partnership. He also has to look after the 150 sheep the National Trust keep on Farleton Fell, and wishes he didn't.

ST JAMES, BURTON

This poignant gravestone caught our eye: "Sacred to the memory of Ernest Baldwin, Private 2/5th Batt. Royal Lancaster Regiment ("The King's Own") died from illness contracted on active service June 16th 1919 aged 28. Also of Pte Albert Baldwin, 45th compy. Machine gun corp, who fell in action August 23rd 1917. And of Margaret Baldwin mother of the above who died February 26th 1907 aged 52 years. Also John Baldwin her husband who died January 29th 1938 aged 82 years."

BURTON MSA NORTH

We were kind of running out of steam when we reached here, thinking what can we say about this motorway service area to make it interesting and special. We noted down the details of the "Made in Cumbria" stall inside the shop "selling crafts and gifts for every occasion - hand-crafted in Cumbria to a high standard for the Kendal-based council initiative." Then we met the new manager, John Wilkie, who told us Princes Harry and William had recently been on site, en route to the Lake District. And so, at a stroke, Moto's Burton won our famous visitor award.

LANCASTER CANAL

Considering the hills and the east-west run of the rivers, it was always an exceptionally ambitious plan to try to create a canal from Lancaster to the Lancashire coalfields and also north into the Lake District, but they had a damn good stab at it. They got from here down to Preston between 1792 and 1799 and up to Kendal by 1819. And when the Lancaster-Preston Railway opened, they cut their prices to maintain cargo carriage. The route of the canal swings briefly eastward south of here down the line of the Tewitfield Locks. The canal is not currently passable immediately either side of the locks.

TRUCKHAVEN

There's a short arm of motorway standard running north-west from the M6 here to a big truckers facility: motel, restaurant and shop. The high security lorry compound can accommodate 300 vehicles and is monitored by 25 CCTV cameras. TNT driver John, taking Kingsmill Bread north from West Brom reckons: "excellent food always, relaxing atmosphere, good overnight stop".

Cumbria

A short and snappy new name for what was Westmorland and Cumberland. Big county, huge hills and lakes, small population.

J35

THE HONOURABLE SOCIETY OF TRADE PLATERS

You know those blokes who stand on slip roads with a car number plate in their hand, trying to hitch a lift. Well, we had the pleasure of meeting one of them who explained to us what they are up to. Chris Guy delivered the Rover 45 which MG Rover kindly provided us with to undertake our field research.

Chris lives in Banbury and had risen at 5.30 in the morning to get the car to us in Worcestershire by 9.30 am. He then needed to reach British Car Auctions in Tewkesbury to pick up his next vehicle. I cannot imagine how one would hitchhike from a village on the Worcester-Hereford border to Tewkesbury, and there's only one bus a day into Worcester itself. Chris tries not to use taxis or even public transport as that all eats into his income for the day. He works for a company based in the north of England who do nothing but plot the logistics of delivering individual vehicles – cars, vans and lorries – between locations. Mostly they are re-possessed vehicles, so a brand new Rover 45 was unusual for him. The firm work out his day's duties and estimate travel times, but it is entirely up to him to get from drop-off point to next pick-up point.

TV MAST

One of 2,500 structures providing broadcast signals operated by Crown Castle, which used to be the BBC Home Service transmission division before the Beeb sold off that aspect of their work in 1997. Crown Castle is an American communications business, and they recently handed over the British infrastructure to National Grid Transco for £1.1 billion.

You can be sure someone's made a fortune from the disposal of assets that used to be in the public sector.

RIVER LUNE

Here the river is reaching the end of its long sweep west south of Kirkby Lonsdale. It cuts round the north edge of Lancaster, and, though only three miles from Morecambe, doesn't then enter the sea but drops again southward before swinging west near the University site to flow into Fleetwood Bay. There are good footpaths and cycleways along the 15km Millennium Park.

7920

7888

HOLIDAY INN

Can I help you, sir? Yes, tell me the name of the most famous person ever to have stayed here. Darren Campbell. Who? The runner. That dwarf out of Lord of the Rings. What's he called? I don't know. Fun Loving Criminals. Oh yes, I've heard of them. Mark Owen of Take That. Right. That actor from Four Weddings. Hugh Grant? No, the other one – who made the speech. Simon Callow? No, John Hannah. Rory Underwood. Oh yeah. What about Belinda Carlisle? Right, she'll do, thanks.

J34

The Lake District

Mountain sports firms in the area have recently been campaigning to resist the application of EU safety-at-heights regulations to mountain climbing. The implication is that red and yellow warning signs, scaffolding and air bags would have to be installed along Scafell crag and other popular climbing sites.

TEWITFIELD

Immediately east of the carriageway are the only 8 locks on the 57 mile northern stretch of the Lancaster Canal. Passengers disembarked and walked the towpath (rising 75 feet over three-quarters of a mile) between the levels allowing the canal company to claim an average speed of 10 mph along its whole length. They could refresh themselves at a small inn that is now the stylish, contemporary Longlands Hotel and Restaurant, the latter of which we can recommend.

BORWICK WATERS

British Waterways have recently invested £200,000 to turn this hole full of water that was a source of gravel for the M6 into a fishing facility. They have spent £30,000 on stocking various ponds with various fish – including carp, golden orfe, golden rudd, golden tench, dace, chub and barbel. Angling Times has been monitoring efforts at the 25 acres, which they reckon have gone from looking like a bomb site to a "superwater".

MORECAMBE-LEEDS LINE

The famous Settle-Carlisle Railway is the top two-thirds of a route that extends down past Settle and Skipton to Leeds. South of Settle, it connects with this branch line that runs west to Morecambe. Five services a day will take you through Carnforth station to the west where – wait for it – many of the key scenes of the famous and timeless Noel Coward "Brief Encounter" film were shot with Celia Johnson and Trevor Howard.

Carnforth

The Editor was driven by his son, Ben, along the length of the M6 in both directions one weekend to assess its capacity to become a book. They rested and refreshed at the County Hotel here, a pleasingly independent institution, and found the local bookshop, which showed interest in carrying the planned title. The Courier, the town's free newspaper, reported that Philip Jones Opticians had won the Start-Up Practice of the Year in the Opticians Awards, "one of the biggest nights in the optical calendar".

Kirkby Lonsdale

In 1860 William Whellan of Pontefract published his History and Topography of the Counties of Cumberland and Westmoreland: "comprising their ancient and modern history, a general view of their physical character, trade, commerce, manufactures, agricultural condition," statistics etc etc. Of this place he assessed its area as 8,098 acres with a rateable value of £7,001 4s 3d.

The manor was sold by Queen Mary to Thomas Carus of the Middle Temple in 1557, then changed hands several times before reaching Sir John Lowther, "ancestor of the present possessor, the Earl of Lonsdale, who has the tolls and control of the market and fair at Kirkby, and holds a court leet and view of frank pledge annually in October." In the Samling restaurant at Mansergh Hall, they'll rustle you up a braised pig's head. Cumbria Life explained how: "What you need: 1 pig's head, spilt into two down the centre. What you do: Bring it to the boil from cold three times, refreshing after each. Burn off the excess hair with a blow torch."

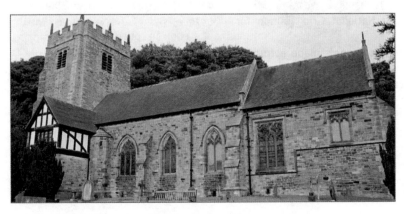

ST WILFRED'S, HALTON

The most prominent stone in the graveyard reads: "In memory of Mary, the beloved wife of Thomas Norman of Halton who died August 25th 1861 aged 51 years. Husband, I die – my peace is won, I linger, but my race is run. Oh, choose a grave where I may sleep Untroubled. Where thou, perchance at evening's hour may'st o'er my head-stone drop a flower." Thomas had 14 years to drop those flowers.

TRAVEL INN

Across the road from this branch is a vast exercise emporium called Total Fitness. Classes include Begin 2 Spin, Step 2 the Max, Absolute ABS, Wow Workout, Barbell Blast and Nuclear Circuit. Or you can "purchase your Fit Balls from Reception and reap the rewards of training in the comfort of your own home and at your convenience."

MOOR HOSPITAL

This was the County Lunatic Asylum. Peter Williamson's celebration of "the life of a great institution from 1816 to 2000" notes that some patients spent their lives here as did many members of staff, and for many it became a family affair. To them it was much more than a hospital – it was home. Early inmates' memories can't have been so cosy. An 1841 report described thirty patients "chained down during the day-time on seats so constructed as to answer all the purposes of water closets."

ASHTON MEMORIAL

Commissioned by Lancaster-lad-made-good Lord Ashton as a tribute to one of his late wives. Completed in 1909, it sits in 54 acres of parkland that includes a botanical Palm House full of butterflies. Inside the folly is an art gallery, and round the edge a viewing platform, and to top it all, you can get married in the building.

HEYSHAM NUCLEAR POWER STATIONS

Not just one but two nuclear power stations on the horizon, down by the beach. Friends of the Earth and the Lancaster and District Green Party have been lobbying for Heysham 2 be shut down because of a history of technical problems with gas circulator impellers.

LANCASTER UNIVERSITY

In the summer of 2004 they were seeking a new Professor for the Department of Psychology, which has its own Transcranial Magnetic Stimulation facility, and a Chair in Women's Studies who has a background in postcolonial, critical race, transnational gender and sexuality studies.

BIG CHANGE

"People are travelling much longer distances than in the past partly because they can now afford to do so and partly because they have to."

Travel will have to become more local, less frequent, less energy-intensive and slower, if we are to save the planet, says Mayer Hillman in his book.

"We need a less mobile society, which is the reverse of the one the public wish for and which politicians and industry are planning for".

ST JOHN THE EVANGELIST, ELLEL

At its portal, the Reverend John Mackay has advised: "Enter this door as if the floor were gold. And every wall of jewels all of wealth untold. As if a choir in robes of fire were singing here. Nor shout nor rush but hush For God is here."

GALGATE SILK MILL

The original mill dates from 1792 and relied on water to spin silk. The brick chimney was added in 1852. John Champness's book on Lancashire's Architectural Heritage notes that the building's corner pilasters were an early example of mill owners taking thought about external appearances.

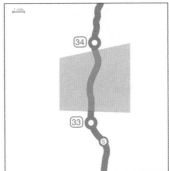

Morecambe

The Belle Vue Hotel has: Lift to all floors, 40 bedrooms with teasmaids, en suite with colour TV, spacious bar with mighty Wurlitzer, extra large dance floor, resident band, varied entertainment programme and large patio garden overlooking the sea. Excellent home cooked cuisine. B&B rates £28 - £30 per person.

Morecambe Bay

Instead of all the gloomy stuff about drowned illegal Chinese immigrant cockle pickers, we turned to Peter Cherry's celebratory coffee table book, full of fabulous photographs: "One of the last wildernesses in England to remain unchanged by man. A sand plain of one hundred square miles and more is revealed twice each day by the ebbing tide which carves the surface into subtly different reliefs each time."

LINOLEUM MAN

Lord Ashton gave his home town lots of employment, the country lots of Williamson oil cloth and linoleum, and the Liberal Party lots of money. "The way in which he dominated a firm, a town and an industry must be seen as an unusually austere, egocentric version of an industrial patriotism which was such a potent force in the society of his youth," writes historian Philip Gooderson.

WEST VIEW FARM

Jim and Susan Holmes allow their beef cattle to live as natural a life as possible before slaughter. Their B&B business has been going 16 years, with most customers coming from the University: odd professors on odd nights. They haven't got over "Roger the Dodger" who kept extending his stay and then disappeared without trace without paying.

THE THREE SIRENS

As we took our snap of the Heysham nuclear plants from here, we watched three pretty girls aged about 15 walk on to the bridge then stop and wave at lorry drivers. This got some horns blasting. Then the girls began dancing and adopting provocative poses for the benefit of the drivers roaring underneath. This stimulated a long succession of horns. Then the girls walked on. They told us they always do that when passing this way.

Lancaster

Like a lot of cities, it's hugely different between day and evening. As we walked to the library we were aware of fine stone buildings and a struggle to find a route for motor traffic around the hills. Later, looking for somewhere to eat in the evening, the place seemed dominated by cavernous but mostly empty bars, presumably patronised by students in term time.

We are put to shame by J.M.W. Turner's magnificent paintings of the area created after his tour of North Lancashire and available as postcards from the Tourist Shop.

THE BARN, BARROW GREAVES

Despite the six cars on the drive, we couldn't raise anyone here, and they haven't responded to the letter we left. They have an excellent view of the motorway, and, beyond it, on the horizon, can see the blocks of flats being erected on the Lancaster University campus aimed at accommodating foreign students who are apparently often worth more financially to the University than their British counterparts, even if their comprehension of English is often not as strong.

C & M MOTORS

Andrew Cornthwaite has operated this vehicle repair and insurance recovery centre since 1973. On one occasion a Renault 5 crashed straight off the motorway and landed upside down in his yard. The driver got out with blood all over his head demanding an ambulance for his wife who was still inside.

THE HONEYCOMB COMPANY

They are busy bees here, importing, blending and packing honey from all over the world to sell to both retail and catering outlets. It's a family business that began with a few hives back in 1947. The big coloured drums are full of imported honey.

Heysham

The port is run by Mersey Docks and handles 250,000 tonnes of general cargo and 420,000 RoRo units. There's talk of bridging the mouth of the Lune to take a trunk road from junction 33 or reintroducing rail freight services to lessen the number of lorries trying to get round Lancaster.

SPOTTING HOLIDAY

Near here we met William, a teenager from Tewkesbury in Gloucestershire, lorry spotting. He was on holiday with his parents at Southport. They'd dropped him off at a footbridge for the day to add to his 12,000 collection gathered over 4 years. His proudest period to date was when he had spotted every one of the 40-odd Ralph Davies liveries from Cheltenham before new registrations were added to that fleet.

FOXHOLES

This distinctive building has had a variety of functions since it stopped being a private house. It has been a hotel and a restaurant and an old people's home. It was semi-derelict for several years until a developer called in Blackpool's top painting and decorating firm to refurbish it – so it can become a private home again.

FORTON SERVICES NORTH

An old motorway construction worker told us the original plan had been to make the flying platform into a motel, but it was launched as a restaurant with an open sun deck above by Top Rank in 1965. Now everything happens down below. There's a 'Food from the Fells' deli. Lancashire cheese and potted shrimps are their best sellers.

RIVER WYRE

A couple of miles east (yes, on the right hand page beyond Dainty's Haulage site) is the Duchy of Lancaster's Wyreside Lakes Fishery, run by Bob and Elaine Birkin, who once met their landlord, the Queen, at a Buckingham Palace Garden Party, and who once had a visit from Prince Charles.

SCORTON ST PETER

This church was built in 1879 and is dedicated to Peter Ormrod, who patronised the locals in Victorian times. A Bolton businessman, he took a fancy to the district and bought up a tract of land from the Duke of Hamilton's estate to create Wyresdale Park. Outside the village shop is a state-of-the-art Lancashire Information Network Kiosk Service touch-screen and phone – weird, unsatisfactory and no match for Garstang's cheerfully manned tourist office.

ADEC ELECTRICS

They've got a new purpose-built headquarters for undertaking electrical installation work for clients ranging from West Lancashire District Council, Subway sandwich counters, Clarks shoe shops and the United North West Co-op. They've been at it for a decade and the owner lives just across the other side of the motorway so he can keep an eye on his premises from home.

WEST LANCS CARAVANS

They don't sell caravans, but store big, utilitarian mobile homes and rent them to caravan sites or to contractors for accommodation for their temporary employees.

HAMPTON HOUSE

We were amongst the last visitors to enjoy a night's accommodation here in its role as a hotel, because it will soon become a care home, after the owners have given up trying to maintain its hotel role in the light of the lack of Americans, and conference competition from the modern city ring road chains.

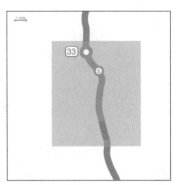

STONE BARN

This is what's called a bank barn, designed so that the animals could be fed from the loft above. The owner has invested a lot of time and money into refurbishing it. He toyed with trying to turn it into a holiday home but it's far too close to the overhead power lines for that. He has been aggravated over the years by thieves pinching slates from the roof and stones from the walls but he now has measures in place to make sure that can't happen again.

FORTON SERVICES SOUTH

They have been Fish Retail Regional Champions. That's nothing to do with seafood: it stands for Friendly Interactive Smile Helpful. On another occasion it was judged Retail Hot Spot. They were Team of the Quarter in September 2002, and got more Moto monthly Fish awards in 2003. In the Truckers Rest Area, the notice on the board says: "Fancy a game of cards or dominos? For a £1 deposit collect a game from the retail shop." More fish?

DAINTY'S HAULAGE

"An eyesore" was the proprietor's opinion of his premises. He used to be a farmer but diversified into heavy haulage and plant hire 15 years ago. Covered in oil and sweat John S. Dainty emerged from under an uplifted lorry cab to tell us of his frustrations with the council, who won't let him pursue his plans. What he likes best is his relationship with his wife, "Head of the Diplomatic Corps."

"DISCOURTEOUS"

A couple of motorway police patrol officers responsible for this stretch told us that the biggest problem around here was not speed but discourteous driving: occupying the middle lane when the near side is empty; not indicating, tail-gating, not tying down loads properly - motorists taking action with no thought for the consequences, "and we literally have to pick up the pieces". The officers used to be just reactive, but now they are pro-active. Thanks to number-plate recognition technology and "good old-fashioned bobbying", they had just tracked down some armed robbers.

BAILTON'S FARM

When we called, Mr Hall, in his 80s, was edging around his yard with a huge, heavy chemical tank on his back, spraying the cobblestones. He rents his fields out to neighbouring farmers, who let their sheep graze on his land. He's angry about the Highways Agency's plan to re-build his access bridge over the motorway to his fields beyond. This was part of the Barnacre estate, which managed to persuade the original motorway planners to erect a dedicated access bridge for every one of their farms north of here. After 40 years' service, some will now be replaced or removed.

MILES

AP

Assured Performance Group are the Air Brake people. They re-manufacture brake actuators, valves, compressors and assemblies for HGV and PSV applications. That means they provide replacement brake units for lorries and buses, and number Stagecoach and Arriva amongst their customers.

KENLIS ARMS (N.O.)

A Victorian hotel seemingly miles from anywhere. But it actually lies close to the Lancaster Canal which brought it custom, and then the railway came along and there was a station nearby which delivered more visitors (including Blackpool stars avoiding the Blitz). It's got the railway on one side and the motorway on the other. So one is constantly aware of the haar of motorway noise, occasionally overlaid by a haarsh of a train passing through. It was cluttered, but cosy, with collections of teapots, brass, books and kids' toys occupying plenty of space.

GARSTANG MAINTENANCE COMPOUND

50 staff, 3 gritters, 2 mobile variable message signs and some Incident Support Units operate from here. On site are 1,000 tonnes of salt and 100 metres of replacement safety barrier, plus 1,000 temporary traffic signs and 4,000 traffic cones.

DUCKETTS FARM FOOTBRIDGE

The Editor was reminded of his childhood Hornby Dublo electric train set on seeing these neat, metal railway footbridges along here. Not that he had one for his set, but he aspired to acquire one, and he knew lucky boys who were proud owners of such a model bridge.

Lytham

Visitors are welcomed by Councillor John Longstaff, Mayor of Fylde, who points out that "as the venue for last year's Weetabix Women's British Golf Open, we proved, once again, that we are specialist in providing quality accommodation and family entertainment on a truly international scale".

Fleetwood

Sits above Blackpool on the peninsula created by the River Wyre, which separates it from Knott End. For a flavour of Fleetwood's noble fishing traditions, invest some time in visiting www.nettingthebay.org.uk, one of the most pleasing and enlightening sites we have encountered.

ROYAL MAIL

1 million items of mail a day are handled here, for the post code areas of Preston (PR), Fylde (FY), Blackburn (BB) and Lancaster (LA). Royal Mail recently claimed to be losing 5p on every first class letter delivered and 9p on second class letters, despite making profits of over £40 million last year.

CPC

This place sells a million and one electronic things. Well, okay, maybe not that many, but it's not far short, because their catalogue runs to 2,832 pages. Let's take a typical page: Doorspy with intercom, Video recorder, Multi-function printer, CD Repair system, prismatic batteries, cordless telephone, battery tester, pen type oscilloscope and wireless optical mouse. That's nine items, multiplied by 3,000 takes it to 27,000. Okay, this place sells 27,000 electronic things.

7648

7616

2.5

J32

7541

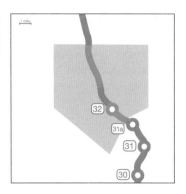

This lovely little town was declared the world's first Fair Trade Town on 27th April 2000. A number of shops agreed to display products from the Third World with Fair Trade marks on them. Purchasing such goods ensures a better deal for the Third World producers. The project was initiated by the local Oxfam group and sponsored by the Co-op, and TV actor and presenter Tony Robinson unveiled a plaque to commemorate the occasion outside the Discovery Centre.

RIVER CALDER

Calder Fell is one of the hills on Bleasdale Moors to our east, 429 metres above sea level. The river runs west into the Wyre south of Garstang.

CAPTAIN CHEVRON

Auto Express magazine in August 2004, as part of their National Motorway Month, introduced us to Captain Chevron who can help reduce tail-gating. A coupon invited readers to vote Yes or No for Captain Chevron, the super-hero who can paint more inverted Vs down the carriageways.

CLAUGHTON MEMORIAL HALL (S.O.)

Tiny village, huge hall - that will take up to 250 people. Could this be anything to do with the man who is commemorated by a seat outside: Councillor Michael Fitzherbert-Brockholes, OBE, JP, DL, KCSG, in recognition of his valuable contributions as a councillor for 35 years? With a name like that, you can imagine he had the clout to get things done. The Parishioners – well, some of them – paid for the seat.

RIVER BROCK

This runs from Holme House Fell on the Bleasdale Moors across to the Wyre a few miles before the Wyre swings north to form an estuary south of Fleetwood.

RABY'S FARM

Ian Stuart has 90 cows producing milk for Dewlay Cheese which is sold all over the world; but that doesn't generate enough income so he's diversified into buying and selling trucks. Twenty dairy farms in the district have gone out of business in the last few years. The motorway cut this farm in two but he can't persuade the Highways Agency or the Council to provide double-glazing or trees to muffle the noise. Most disturbing is when it stops. That means there's been an accident somewhere nearby.

MILES

Blackpool

A company called Leisure Parcs is hoping to get government approval to build a Las Vegas-style casino hotel in the town soon. Cynics of New Labour say the relaxation of gambling laws is one of the few areas where the party has been truly radical. Meanwhile a twenty-four year old Russian has recently bought the TVR sports car firm here.

You can buy replica guns at shops on the promenade. Dozens of the realistic-looking weapons are subsequently confiscated at Blackpool airport every week by people trying to fly them home as souvenirs.

Pleasure Beach	Tower	Zoo	Sandcastle
Geoffrey Thompson, ex-managing director of the Pleasure Beach, died on 12th June 2004. Less than a fortnight later his 101-year old mother Doris passed away. She had preceded him in building the rides to their hair-raising standards.	As you head along the M55 you can start to see the Tower in the distance – over 500 feet in height, and where W.C. Fields worked as a juggler before the First World War.	They've got 1,000 animals in 32 acres, an improvement in animal welfare terms over the days when animals performed in the Tower circus.	Not sand, but hygienically controlled water – 35 fun, interactive features including cannons, magic jets, blasters and a white knuckle chute.

7531

PRESTON NORTH END

We thought at first their National Football Museum was a bit of a cheek, but closer examination of the case to represent the national game next to their ground seemed justified when we discovered Bill Shankly (Liverpool's legendary manager) had played here in the 1930s and 40s (having come from Carlisle), and the even more legendary Tom Finney played here for 14 seasons from 1946, scoring 210 goals for them as well as 30 for England. Matt Busby reckoned Finney was "the closest there has ever been to one man being bigger than a club." Oh yeah, and they were first-ever League winners in 1889.

FLASH FLOOD

In August 2004 we encountered a thunderstorm on the motorway that caused a flash flood across the carriageways, which were overwhelmed with the volume of water. The fast lane was a good nine inches deep in places. Most drivers moved to the middle lane but some people saw fit to carry on regardless.

Burnley

Steve Dealler of the Pathology Laboratory at the General Hospital has devoted considerable energy, intelligence and passion to documenting the state of scientific knowledge on transmissible spongiform encephalopathy.

See the state of play on mad cow disease and its implications for meat-eaters at www.bse.airtime.co.uk. The site is constantly under construction.

Blackburn

The Rovers' supporters club keeps careful note of the timescale of their side's fortunes, particularly in comparison to arch rivals Burnley. "It's 128 years since the Blackburn Rovers were formed and 25 years since they last lost to Burnley in the League. It's 90 years since Burnley won a domestic cup final and 37 years since they last played in Europe." So, no gloating there then.

TICKLED TROUT

They've got a fancy framed certificate in the foyer explaining in toadying language how "We, Sir Malcolm Rognvald Innes of Edinburgh, Knight Commander of the Royal Victorian Order" etc., etc., came up with the coat of arms design: "according to the Law of Arms Know Ye Therefore that we have devised and do by these presents Assign, Ratify and Confirm... the following Ensigns Armorial..." and so on and so forth. It must be a really good place because a small pot of coffee (a cup and a half) cost us £3.75.

LANCASHIRE MOTORWAY POLICE HQ

This was opened on 22nd December 1999 by the Chairman of the Lancashire Police Authority, Dr R.B. Henig JP, and Mrs P.A. Clare, Chief Constable. There are plaques on the wall inside remembering officers killed whilst attending Road Traffic Incidents, and one officer murdered in the course of his duties. When we called we were given a copy of their somewhat bizarre 2002 comic calendar full of pictures of motorway accidents with semi-amusing and appropriate slogans alongside. January shows a burnt-out truck next to "Arrive Alive" and it goes downhill from there.

Longridge

Plenty of praise for the golf club: "one of the most picturesque rounds in the county" and "best value for money in Lancashire". Dave Taylor reckoned it was "the best course in the UK for this price. The only negative is the lack of signs to the next tee".

RIVER DARWEN

Walton Mill was driven by the Darwen which runs into the Ribble near the centre of Preston. Walton summit to the south defeated the Lancaster Canal builders, who had to substitute the waterway with a horse-drawn tram to its short South section that joins the Leeds-Liverpool Canal.

TRAVEL INN

The Preston east site has a Brewsters Norman Jepson pub alongside containing a Fun Factory for kids. Norman Jepson (1945-1999) was a Whitbread executive, responsible for the development of this site, who died suddenly before it was completed. It opened in 2000 and so far their most famous guest has been Tony Hadley of Spandau Ballet and populist TV drama.

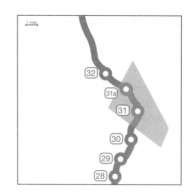

HOLLYWOOD EXPRESS

One fifth of the popcorn consumed by British film fans is produced here. They also ship out sweets, hot dogs, nachos, ice cream and janitorial disposables to cinemas all over the country in unique vehicles with separate ambient, chilled, frozen and chemicals compartments.

TARMAC

The leading supplier of aggregates, mortar, concrete blocks and asphalt in the UK, with 10,000 employees worldwide generating a turnover of £1.4 billion.

BALFOUR BEATTY UTILITIES

They maintain, repair and rehabilitate water pipes, sewers and gas pipes, which means they issue 38 notices of digging up a road somewhere every hour of the day and night.

BROCKHOLES

Kevin Clarke has been extracting sand and gravel here for Hansons for the last 15 years and is now looking forward to doing something different. He has helped the site win a series of environmental awards over the last decade. It's a member of the Quarry Products Association Good Neighbours Scheme, which means it endeavours to abide by pledges to reduce the impact of operations, make a positive contribution to the environment and keep the wheels clean on lorries. It's soon to close.

RIVER RIBBLE

Bird watchers Bill and Robin were delighted to learn that the Brockholes Sand and Gravel pits will close next year. On the lakes to the north of the river in the last two years they have spotted 130 species. Most common: lapwing and most rare: spoonbill, garganey and semi-palmated sandpiper.

"YOU'VE NEVER HAD IT SO GOOD"

This is the original motorway opening commemorative structure. Sadly, it's not sitting in its original setting but has been moved to accommodate the widening and the modifications around what is now junction 31 of the M6. It's just to the north of the Police Headquarters off the west-bound A677. There's no pedestrian access, so we don't recommend a visit. You might be hit by a car.

HIGHER WALTON MILL

This was built in 1860. Up on the third floor are 400 pianos. They are mostly refurbished second-hand English and German instruments, though the company, Dales, also sell some new pianos from Korea, Japan and China. It's the biggest second-hand piano business in the North West.

Clitheroe

Based at the Old Bakehouse Gallery is artist Peter Taylor, who specialises in big sky/big sea landscapes – but with a difference. The sea is distinctly scary. Lancashire Life gave readers a flavour: Surfing Noah shows a tiny ark about to be overwhelmed by a giant wave; and The Big One has Blackpool's Big Dipper slammed by another massive breaker. Yeah, we know climate change will soon destroy the planet, but do we want previews in paintings?

BAMBER BRIDGE MILL

This was built in 1905 and closed in 1959. In its heyday it ran 130,000 spindles. Bamber Bridge's big claim to fame came in the Second World War when some American troops were stationed in a nearby village. White and black troops were strictly segregated in the American army at this time. Black troops got on well with the locals and were drinking in a pub on a Saturday night when white US Military Policemen tried to arrest them. White Lancashire soldiers and locals intervened and a skirmish ensued that saw one black American die and several dishonourably discharged and sentenced to hard labour.

Preston

David Hindle's "Twice Nightly" charts the rise and fall of Preston's popular music hall traditions, the final curtain being Pat Phoenix ("Elsie Tanner from Coronation Street") declaring the Empire a bingo club in 1964. In 1995 Preston had 105 real ale pubs, now there are only 45, reports Ale Cry, the CAMRA West Lancs newsletter. In the summer of 2004, the Museum was running a travelling "Grin Up North" exhibition: "Discover the roots of northern humour, take a journey through the Hall of Fun; stimulate your senses in the Laughter Lab". And adding to entertainment, the place is home of Northwest Books, who cheerfully take our titles to many shops.

SAUSAGE COUNTRY

One of the most elaborate leaflets we came across on our travels was "Serious about Sausages" funded by a host of agencies with a vested interest in pushing food or business in the North West. It's thirty pages thick with a fold-out map that suggests sausage production is particularly clustered in this vicinity.

LEYLAND ST AMBROSE

A long drive from Worcestershire brought us directly here, where we read on the big noticeboard "Ask and it will be given to you, Seek and you will find, Knock and the door will be opened to you" (Matt 7:7), which we took to be a good omen for our researches in this area as we continued heading north exploring the sights left and right.

JARVIS HOTEL

Built into the wall next to reception is a glass-fronted box containing a bottle of Napoleon old liqueur cognac. The adjoining plaque says: "This hotel was opened 1st September 1980 and this casket will be opened on 1st September 2030 and the brandy will be served by the manager to his guests." Best guest so far: Carol Vorderman. And Tony Blair popped in once to address a Labour meeting.

J30

J29

J28

ALL SAINTS, HIGHER WALTON

One of the biggest stones reads: "Sacred to the Memory of John Clitheroe who departed this life December 1st 1868 aged 62 years. A faithful friend, a husband dear, a tender father sleepeth here. Great is the loss that we sustain but hope in heaven to meet again." His widow, Ellen, had to wait 22 years, until she was 80 for this to happen.

M61

This runs south-east from here (with an all-ways junction at the M65 just 2 miles on) down towards Manchester.

PRESTON-BLACKBURN

In the early 1820s Thomas Gray wrote a book entitled "Observations on a General Iron Railway to supercede the necessity of Horses in all Public Vehicles." He lobbied Parliament to trial a line between Liverpool and Manchester and was branded a madman for his idiotic enthusiasm for such an unrealistic means of transport.

BOCM PAULS

Preston Mill sits in a triangle created by the M6, the M61 and the M65 running east from Junction 29 past Blackburn and on to Burnley. "For credit control, cattle, Press 1, for management services, cattle, press 2, for mill operations, pig and poultry, press 3, for electrical engineering, press 4, for mechanical engineering, press 5. Thank you." BOCM stands for British Oil and Cake Mills.

NOVOTEL

Our road tester Pete Mitchelson tells us every one is identical, with the same furniture imported from Paris. Unlike the Tickled Trout up the road, their idea of two cups of coffee are mugs with a huge pot you can hardly lift off the table, from which you help yourself for £3.20.

PRESTON BY-PASS

The works were inaugurated by the Right Hon Hugh Molson M.P., Joint Parliamentary Secretary of the Ministry of Transport and Civil Aviation, on 12 June 1956. Upon its opening, the Department noted this "guinea pig... marks the beginning of a new era of motoring in Britain. It is the first link in a network of motorways, which, progressively completed, will contribute to an increasing extent to the health of the community and to the national economy. The national motorways in general and the Preston By-pass in particular are designed to enable traffic to travel safely at high speeds, and to minimise the chance of accidents arising from bad driving. These objectives are achieved principally by: (a) the prohibition of pedestrians, cyclists and animals; (b) the prohibition of access from adjacent land; (c) dual carriageways separated by a central reservation; (d) the provision at junctions of acceleration and deceleration lanes; (e) the adoption of easy gradients and very large radius curves; (f) the provision of hard shoulders on the nearside of the carriageway for use in emergency halts: and (g) sign posts of a size which can be read both by day and by night without the need for the driver to slow down."

Chorley

Jack Smith's book on this place in the fifties commences by recounting at some length the many fights that began in the basement snooker hall under the Royal picture palace, in which he was sometimes involved: "It wasn't too bad getting hit with the thick end of a snooker cue - it was the solid ivory balls which hurt most of all especially if they hit you in the face or on the back of the head." In the 1990s this fighting spirit amongst locals was channelled into the Save the Heart of Lancashire Campaign to resist an extension of the M65 through the Chorley North East Green Belt, well documented in Simon Jones's book "The Battle for Lancashire's Future".

CHRIS'S BRITISH ROADS

For loads of fantastic information about every aspect of the British road scene we recommend you take a leisurely visit to www.cbrd.co.uk where Chris Marshall has spent a lot of time and effort compiling facts, figures, anecdotes, advice and opinions on many thoroughfares. For us the best bit is a lovingly presented reproduction of every page of the official Opening Brochure for the Preston By-Pass. It's got photographs of the officials and aerial views of the roundabouts during and after construction.

BRITISH COMMERCIAL VEHICLE MUSEUM

We were delighted with this place that offers a nostalgic trip especially to those who were born in the same year that the Bedford OL AD first took to the road (the one here is exquisitely presented in Bibby's of Ingleton livery complete with milk churns on the back). It's the largest commercial vehicles museum in Europe, housed in Leyland's old King Street building. They've got buses, vans, fire engines and war-time vehicles from many marques – not just those of Leyland - and all in mint condition.

Leyland

It's where lots of lorries have come from.

James Sumner, son of a blacksmith, started with steam wagons in 1884, then made tricycles for a while. A powered lawn mower proved a big hit at the Royal Lancashire Agricultural Show, after which he tried sticking one of the lawn mower engines in a three-wheeled car for Theodore Carr of Carrs Biscuits of Carlisle, at which point he realised he was on to something. In partnership with the Spurrier family from Manchester, the Lancashire Steam Motor Company was formed in 1896. Thousands of petrol and diesel powered vehicles, including tanks, emerged from Leyland Motor Corporation plants over the next 100 years.

It became part of British Leyland from 1968, then Leyland Trucks in the 1980s.

WIGAN-PRESTON MAIN LINE

To explain the service alterations for the West Coast Route Modernisation August Bank Holiday Engineering Work between 28th August and 5th September 2004, Virgin issued a 96 page A5-size book of timetable amendments.

CAMELOT (S.O.)

This seems like a really good place to take kids of all ages for a fun day; at £15 for an adult to enter. The Editor fearlessly made his way to the Gauntlett at the far end and climbed aboard the ride that rose steadily up a long track before commencing its hair-raising descent and yawing through bends and loops that kept him hanging on to his seat with one hand and his camera with the other.

CHARNOCK RICHARD NORTH SERVICES

An attractive agent for Barclaycard accosted us in reception, as she does everyone who walks across the threshold. She does a four-hour shift with a goal of getting 15 people to sign up for a card in that time. And she is "well paid" if she achieves that figure, which she normally manages to do, though it's "hard work."

ST JOSEPH'S PRIMARY SCHOOL

"Where we work, care and share." On the day we visited, workmen were laying a new circular patio round the back. Their JCB had badly dug up the playing fields whilst filling a skip with rubble; meanwhile they had had their tools stolen from the back of their pick-up truck.

Park Hall

This is a Best Western Hotel with lots of add-ons round the back, including a Spanish-style villa complex, a health club and some auction houses. It's adjacent to Camelot, and we walked through the maintenance compound to get a decent picture of the rides, having previously tried to snatch snaps from the top of the Gauntlet big dipper that looked like nothing on earth.

MICHAEL THEOBALD GARAGE

Air Conditioning Service and Repair, Engine Tuning and Diagnostics, MOT Testing, Fuel Injection Servicing, All Repairs. What more could you want!

BUCKSHAW VILLAGE

2,500 houses and a number of massive distribution warehouses will soon occupy this brown field site that was once a huge Royal Ordnance factory.

Locals still bear a grudge against a government employee who took back-handers that destroyed the military commercial operation. He served 5 years in jail for the offence and is out now, but people roundabout point out that he put 7,000 out of work as a result of his selfishness.

MILES

Lancashire

"Think of Lancashire and if you're a foodie you might think of cheese – the best in the world, or potted shrimps – by Royal Appointment, of course. If you're sporty you might think of Bill Beaumont, Carl Fogarty or Jason Queally – this was his training ground to become Olympic champion. If you're into entertainment you'll conjure up Jane Horrocks, Victoria Wood or Eric Morecambe – Lancastrians are famous for their sense of humour. If you're a historian you'll think of Richard Arkwright's Spinning Jenny – this was where the Industrial revolution all began."

CHARNOCK RICHARD SERVICES SOUTH

There's a KFC and Burger King on the bridge with tables overlooking the carriageways north and south.

And fine, big abstract paintings by Elaine Jones on the stairwells.

COPPULL RING MILL (N.O.)

It was built in 1906 by foremost Lancashire mill architects Stott & Sons of Oldham. Now it's office space, including a regional one for the Church of Jesus Christ Latter Day Saints. The old wages office has become the Red Herring pub, and in the summer of 2004 landlord Steve Cranshaw staged a bikers' charity Do called Hic Bibi (Latin for: Here I drink) to raise money for the Derian House Children's Hospital.

Martin Mere

This is one of 9 centres run by the Wildfowl and Wetland Trust, which has spent £10 million on wetland bird conservation across the world in the last 10 years. Here you can explore the Australian Riverway, the South American lake, and the Oriental pen. You can see Pink-footed geese, Whooper and Beswick's swans and lots of exotic ducks and flamingos. The Pinkfoot Pantry serves snacks, and hot and cold meals. Do these include chicken, we wonder?

MILL LIFE

Philip Gooderson's History of Lancashire describes the daily routine of a millworker through the second half of the 19th and first half of the 20th century: Woken at five with a knock on the bedroom window from the "knocker-up". Walk to the factory for six. Breakfast break at eight. A pie and a jug of ale delivered by the children for his dinner at 12.30. Then home for tripe and onions at five.

By pooling their wages a disciplined family could usually keep their members from the disgrace of the workhouse or crime.

GATHURST GOLF CLUB (N.O.)

This has had to move twice since it teed off in 1913. Ministry of Transport agents arrived on the course in 1959 to begin planning the M6 despite no agreement having been reached with the club which was forced to move to its present site. According to the club's official history, "E.B. Naylor is arguably the most influential and prominent member the club has ever had." A native of Bolton, he was appointed Head of Chemistry at the Wigan Mining and Technical College in 1905 and stayed there 33 years. "A gentleman", he always played golf in plus fours.

DEAN LOCK HOUSE (N.O.)

Mr Wesley successfully bid for this place at auction a couple of years ago when British Waterways decided to sell it off. It sits at the junction between the Douglas navigation and the Leeds-Liverpool canal.

LEEDS LIVERPOOL CANAL

At 127 miles, this is the longest single canal in Britain, linking Skipton, Burnley, Blackburn and Wigan. This bit opened in 1781 and in 1906 was carrying over 2 million tons of goods.

RIVER DOUGLAS

Philip Bagwell and Peter Lyth explain in their excellent book 'Transport in Britain, 1750 – 2000' that the greater part of inland navigation was already engineered and effective before the appearance of the first purpose-built canal across virgin land. Rivers had long been adapted for regular haulage routes. In 1720, Wigan Corporation supported the Parliamentary Bill to approve improvements to this river to make it navigable from Wigan to the Ribble estuary which would be "beneficial to Trade, advantageous to the Poor and convenient for the Carriage of Coals, Cannel, Stone, Slate and other Goods and Merchandizes."

ORRELL HOUSE FARM

Fred Bradburn was 82 in August 2004. His family took on this place in 1935 and bought it in 1951. The farm consists of 205 acres, 12 having been lost to the M6 which turned a couple of square fields into triangles. 100 cows produce for MilkLink. Fred has vivid memories of a runaway tractor that was started up in gear and headed across a field heading for the main road when one of his workers managed to leap aboard and switch it off.

Southport

This place launched plans for the North West Coastal Trail designed to run from Carlisle to Chester "taking in miles of golden sands, dunes, estuaries, and man-made waterfronts, both historic and modern." They hope to have it open by 2012.

Skelmersdale

The aging new town came out at Number 46 in the book of Crap Towns. But as the authors considered Winchester, St. Andrews, Portsmouth, St. John's Wood, Ascot, Brighton, Aldeburgh and Oxford even more crap, maybe it's just a crap book.

Haigh Hall

An 1820 history of Wigan describes the seat of the Crawford and Balcarres family as standing beautifully and occupying one of the best situations in Lancashire. From the Park on a clear day can be seen "thirteen counties of England and Wales, together with the Isle of Man... and the town of Wigan is seen below, as standing upon a hill in the midst of a fine valley."

WIGAN-STOCKPORT

Prior to the 20th century it was common for passenger luggage to be strapped on to the roof of the railway carriages, as had been the tradition with coach travel. Frequently the luggage was piled too high, and it got knocked off by low bridges. These days, to lessen the number of bicycles being carried on commuter trains, rail operators have suggested cyclists keep a bike at either end of their regular rail journey.

Parbold

Take the road to Parbold from Junction 27 and you will pass a sign that says "Welcome to Lancashire – a place where everyone matters", then a sign that says "Welcome to West Lancashire", then a stone wall with a plaque that says "Welcome to Parbold", where we find an excellent map and history of the village on a large board in the "artistic corner" with a gallery, 2 sculptors in an old windmill and the Rocking Horse café.

Standish

The Standish family occupied this place for 700 years until the death of the last in line in the last century. They profited from coal exploited on their estate ever since the 14th century. In 1600 the fuel was used by "divers tradesmen and other handycraft men in Wigan". The last mine in the vicinity was the Robin Hill Drift, which closed in 1963.

VALE ROYAL HOTEL

70 people were having their lunch on a Tuesday when we visited this Brewers Fayre venue "serving Britain's favourite pub food." Some looked like they'd been there too often. In the Gents was an advertising board that included a panel for FemaleFirst lingerie. Wedding lingerie specialists from 30B – 55FF, Ashton-in-Makerfield.

HEINZ

We asked their press office what went on here and they sent us a document that said: "Manufacturing Centre producing quick meals and UK can making, soups, beans, bean meals, puddings, pasta, pasta meals, can-making (sic) mainly for UK and Irish markets. Employees 1,640." Yes, that is how this massive, popular food producer decided to present itself in the M6 Sights Guide. In the paper recently we saw that they have increased the amount of tomato in their Tomato Soup from 74% to 84%, and they've taken out a bit of the salt and sugar, and put the price up from 59p to 79p. If you phone them and are left hanging in mid-air, instead of musak, a voice tells you: "Okay, I'm not much to look at. I'm pretty much your average baked bean..."

Liverpool

WATERFRONT

Local government agents have been trying to sink the term Merseyside for future marketing purposes. "Liverpool is the sizzle that sells the sausage."

MUSEUMS

The Conservation Centre, the Museum of Liverpool Life and the Merseyside Maritime Museum were nationally the top three sites with greatest increases in visitor numbers last year.

FOOTBALL STADIA

The ashes of 800 Everton fans have been buried at Goodison Park since 1989, but the management declared that the practice must cease in 2004. Wayne Rooney got out of town in September 2004.

Meanwhile over at the Liverpool ground, manager Houllier was receiving anonymous death threats in the spring of 2004.

M58

This is a was-it-worth-it sort-of motorway running westward from here via a really strange junction configuration to the A59 Liverpool-Ormskirk Road. Perhaps it keeps some traffic out of Orrell to the north-west of the junction, where branches of the Co-op sell the Morning Worker next to the rest of the newspapers.

LIVERPOOL-WIGAN

A handful of financial institutions, which own nearly all of Britain's trains, are to face a crackdown from the government following complaints that they have a stranglehold over rolling stock and are squeezing grotesque profits out of rail operators, reported the Guardian on its business pages in July 2004.

SANDYFORTH FARM

Doctor Charles Mather gave up medicine to become a farmer and he's addicted to it, despite a bad experience over open-cast mining on the land to the south of the 1678 farmhouse. This was the biggest privately-owned coalmine in the country after nationalisation and delivered half-a-million tonnes between 1996 and 2000, when the owners – "now driving around in Ferraris" – went bust.

"LEAVE SPACE"

Motorway patrol officer David Berry spent 8 years as a policeman on the streets of Manchester dealing with drugs, robbery and rape, before serving on the M6, which was a cultural challenge as he was now involved with nice people in trouble. On the morning we met he had sorted out a lorry which had slewed across the central reservation and ploughed 600 metres into a field without anyone being hurt. The previous day he'd mopped up at a fatality in which a young motorcyclist was almost split in two. He never forgets a fatality and is sometimes told to take counselling. His advice to us all is "leave space between you and the vehicle in front."

Ashton

This place is in the Borough of Wigan, though it doesn't get a mention in the Destination Wigan Visitor Guide. When we rang the Wigan Tourist Information Centre, someone told us that "there is not really a lot there, not that I can think of."

OUR LADY IMMACULATE

The Catholic church of Bryn and Garswood dates from 1903 and contains a memorial to local Martyr St Edmund Arrowsmith, canonised by Pope Paul VI in 1970. Edmund was born in Garswood in 1585, ordained in 1612, and preached until 1628 when he was arrested, then hanged, drawn and quartered.

His right hand is preserved at St. Oswald's, Ashton, and touching it was said to have brought about a number of miraculous cures.

CAR PLANET

The Chief Executive of BMW sees a rosy future for car sales. Helmut Panke told the Detroit Automotive Press Association in August 2004 that there should be 70 million new vehicles (not all BMWs) being sold annually by 2010. He's particularly hopeful that the Chinese, who currently only have 10 vehicles per thousand population, will buy lots more, taking them towards America's magnificent figure of 900 cars for every 1,000 people.

HOW MANY? HOW BIG?

There are almost half a million licensed goods vehicles over 3.5 tonnes on British roads, a third of which are articulated. Total freight movement between 1970 and 2000 rose by more than 80%. Diesel lorries emit nearly 50% of particulates, the main contributor to respiratory illnesses. The RAC recently called for another £20 billion to be spent on roads.

W.H. MALCOLM

A logistics and construction firm employing 1,600 and deploying 450 trucks, 1,000 trailers and over 100 heavy plant machines. A photograph in the foyer remembers the man who made most of it possible: Donald John Malcolm, 16th April 1925 – 3rd May 2003.

EDDIE SPOTTING

The haulage legend has several books to its name. For a reverential account, check out the little 96 page Ian Allan ABC containing 200 pictures of Eddie Stobart vehicles but no photo of the man himself. The fan club is based at Brunthill Road, Kingstown Industrial Estate, Carlisle, Cumbria CA3 0EH.

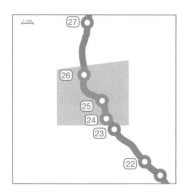

Talk about cashing in on a literary reference. They've surely gone overboard here. There's a pub called the Orwell at Wigan Pier, then there's Wigan Pier itself, which is not a pier but a converted mill full of industrial artefacts and 20th century packaging and marketing materials provided by Robert Opie, who used to run the Packaging Museum at Gloucester Docks. Wigan never had a proper pier - just a canalside jetty. However, we did register a cabinet full of awards for the tourism enterprises.

I took the road to Wigan Pier for what would be a trip down memory lane, because I was interviewed for a job here as a Liberal Studies lecturer at the tech college back in 1970, and hadn't been back since. I approached the place open-minded (as all these exploratory journeys require), but I came away struggling to say something positive. First, there's a weird one-way and overwhelmed traffic system, then, as I walked up to the town from the "Pier", I was accosted by the fattest beggar I've ever seen. I was looking for the old college, and discovered it is now the Town Hall with the library behind it.

A sign inside read: "Verbal Abuse. Intimidating, threatening or inappropriate language or behaviour towards library staff or customers will result in your being asked to leave the premises." A friendly librarian directed me to the History Centre, displaying a modern tapestry illustrating neighbouring townships, an elaborate, colourful community affair - but in danger of deteriorating fast with cleaners brushing carpet dust over the edge of the landing to float down on to the fabrics. My counsel on the inadvisability of this was not well received.

As I walked back to the "Pier" the fat beggar attempted to accost me again. Next day I read that three armed robberies had taken place in Wigan on that day. As an excellent History Centre pamphlet explains, Wigan suffered severely during the Cotton Famine after the American Civil War. Thousands of local workers became dependent on the miserly offerings of the Poor Law.

ST HELENS-WIGAN LINE

In the 1850s intense rivalry between the East Lancashire Railway and the Lancashire-Yorkshire railway resulted in blockades of the Blackburn station. The Blackburn Standard declared: "It is not at all astonishing that railway property should be so depreciated in value in comparison with other investments of this country when we have so constantly exposed to you glaring instances of the reckless and careless manner in which the affairs of different companies are conducted."

HAYDOCK PARK

How do you stop racegoers arriving by car late and not wanting to drive as far as the car park? By putting decorative steel posts 2 feet 6 inches high at 4 feet 6 inch intervals all along the long approach avenue to prevent vehicles parking on the footpath. There are over 300 of them. The course's slogan is "Serious sport, serious fun."

LOMBARD

An office for business customers with turnovers between one and ten million wanting finance leasing. Royal Bank of Scotland's "lending solutions for personal customers" website has a girl with a big grin on her face. Not clear if she's a lender or a lendee.

SPEEDY HIRE

They've £123 million worth of equipment for hire and 800 delivery vehicles and 2,500 "helpful, informed and highly motivated staff" - so the one we spoke to here asking what went on at these offices cannot have been one of that number. However all you need to know is in their big thick brochures.

EDDIE STOBART

His Dad delivered fertiliser to farms in Cumbria. Eddie set up shop in 1970 and now has 1,000 vehicles to his name, a few disguised as Pepsi, Tango or Daily Mirror lorries. Strangely, Eddie shares one job with James Irlam – carrying Coca Cola - apparently too precious a commodity to be assigned to one haulier. This is one of three Control Centres organising logistics well away from the well-known livery, because no lorries occupy this business park.

HAYDOCK GARDEN BUILDINGS

For 20 years they have been retailing wooden garden sheds, play dens and summer houses, prefabricated concrete garages and some greenhouses. Their best seller is the Super Apex 8 ft x 6 ft garden shed made in Yorkshire. They shift a dozen of these each week.

THISTLE HOTEL

Putting the Holiday Inn across the road to shame, staff here could recollect Alex Ferguson, Brian Conley, Kevin Keegan, Jason Donovan and Boy George as past guests. And when we called, a giant photograph of a sexy model in a G-string dominated the lobby designating a Gossard Lingerie event on the premises. We saw no more.

OLD BOSTON TRS

This Telephone Repeater Station was built in the early 1950s to boost all phone connections between Liverpool and Manchester and operate the telephone exchange for Haydock and St Helens. Now all the phone lines are fibre optic cable and just a few technicians are based here.

J23

SHELL SERVICE STATION (N.O.)

Doubtless over the years this site has done great business for users of the East Lancs, but unless you are desperate, don't try to reach it unless you are already on the East Lancs heading east, because you have to try to get off a scary roundabout that takes M6 feeder roads and envelopes the East Lancs itself, with multiple lanes and traffic lights.

SELWYN JONES SPORTS CENTRE

This big orange shed was opened in 1998 by Dave Watts MP, next to Newton-le-Willows Community High School. In Reception was a plastic crate full of apples, pears and bananas, with a sign: "Free fruit (for children) Go on stuff your face. One piece of fruit per person per visit." The receptionist thought Selwyn Jones was a local councillor.

7120

WARRINGTON-WIGAN

A Royal Train once stopped for the night at Wigan railway station. Queen Victoria's man-servant apparently paced the platform continuously and complained to the local staff that the carriages were shaking Her Majesty "like the devil".

LIVERPOOL-MANCHESTER

A three-way junction to the east connects it to the Wigan line.

Bagwell and Lyth describe the state of public transport in Britain as lamentable. "Rather than following the example of continental Europe, where railways have been properly maintained, British governments adopted the inappropriate model of the United States, which more or less abandoned passenger rail services in the 1950s. As car travel became established as the norm in the 1960s, the British ceased to take their railways seriously."

7104

Leigh

A "Leyther" has created a website to educate people from around the world about the town which "had its own corporation until the government realignment in 1974" when it "became governed by Wigan's council and moved from Lancashire to Greater Manchester. Speak to any Leyther however and they will tell you that we are still from Leigh and still Lancastrians."

J22

Newton

There's many a town called Newton and that's because (according to J.D. Marshall's book about Lancashire) fresh colonies of housing had to be constructed close to the mills, which in turn had to occupy what might have been green field sites near rivers. The lack of local civic leadership meant it was often fifty years or more before anyone got round to sticking in some sewers. The early industrial workers' sense of ill-used subordination led to radicalism, trade unionism and machine-breaking in these parts in the 1820s.

HOLIDAY INN

The best guests they could come up with were Martin Clunes, and Kim Marsh from HearSay - presumably on different occasions or in different rooms.

DISTRIBUTION PARKS

To the north west of Junction 23 is one of those massive new estates of giant sheds which lorries have to reach with goods in transit. This one, which houses W.H. Malcolm, as well as lots of household names, is particularly difficult to find. The Editor stopped at a newsagents for directions and was given a pencil-drawn map by the proprietor, who every day has to aid strangers in this way.

JUNCTION 23

I imagined this would be a place where there'd be a lot of shunts. And as I sat at traffic lights looking warily left and right, imagine what happened. A small van in the next lane rammed on its brakes and skidded to a halt, and behind it a red van tried to do the same thing but too late and hit the back of the white van. I expected the first driver to call me over as a witness but both of them seemed philosophical about the damage to their vehicles.

EAST LANCS ROAD (A580)

The Editor remembers his Dad commuting along here to visit Merseyside building sites. It's a fast dual-carriageway broken up by traffic-lighted junctions, scarred with tyre rubber as the users brake their journeys. Try a trip along it and you'll appreciate how user-friendly the motorways are as a driving medium.

HALF-WAY STAGE

Believe it or not this is the mid-way point of the M6. There are 117 miles to go further north and the same number southward (not including those of the M6 Toll, of course).

Bolton

2004 was the 25th year of the town's festival. Of course not many towns now don't have a summer festival these days. Bolton's distinctive prospects for 8 – 12 year olds included The Wobbly Wire Workshop: create your own clockwork creature from wire, motors, wheels and propellers. We reckon next year they'll have an Olympic gold medalist on site.

THE BULLS HEAD

This is much better than it looks from afar. An attentive, smart manager has everything under control and works fast and effectively in a pleasing bistro-style environment. The signs proclaim high-class gourmet cuisine and innovative ideas, and we are pleased to report that this is what they delivered on the basis of our brief, anonymous visit. Market fresh fish a speciality.

WHITE BUILDING SERVICES

In the yard behind Frederick Stanley House (1925) is a sort of instant garden centre, not so much organically grown from a nursery as a retail outlet for pallet loads of ornaments shipped in from the Far East. At least, that's how it looked to us. And the boss, over in Blackpool, had "no comment."

St Helens

The Council provide a Customer Comments and Suggestions form for their Leisure Centres. There are 60 option boxes to tick as regards the degree to which they are achieving their aims, the top four of which are: Answer the telephone promptly and courteously, Ensure you can find and park at our facilities, Give efficient and prompt service at reception, Treat you in a helpful and friendly manner.

SOUTHWORTH HALL FARM

This was cut up by the arrival of both the M6 and the M62 motorways, and sandstone for M6 bridges was quarried out of the farm land. The holes were filled with builders' waste. It originally belonged to Southworth Hall next door to the north, once home of John Southworth a leading figure in the Roman Catholic faith in this part of the world. The Hall was rebuilt in 1932 and is now on the market for £1 million.

LORRY SPOTTING

Near here we spotted a lorry spotter. Brian Mullin has been at it for 15 years, putting in 20 hours a week. He's noted 16,000 lorry number-plates in that time, which, we told him, didn't seem that many. He's covering 93 liveries, and has binoculars at the ready on a bridge over the carriageway. After five hours you start to see the same vehicles returning in the opposite direction. He shares his interest with Derek, who is disabled, and so has to get his wife to spot for him.

Liverpool

I was responsible for directing an episode of the ITV daytime house clearance show "Everything Must Go Under the Hammer" at Cato Crane's auction house on Merseyside in the summer of 2003. The crew stayed at a hotel built sympathetically into the Albert Dock building, and in the evening my old pal and colleague Michael Dyer of HotBed Media in Birmingham set off with me to find a suitable place for supper. We were both astounded that Liverpool won the European City of Culture title over Birmingham on the basis of what we encountered. But others describe it as "the new Barcelona".

J21A

DATEL

They are the UK's leading independent supplier of business management systems, providing "best of breed" products from Sage, Microsoft and IBM. They employ 100 people. One IT customer is quoted as saying: "Datel is almost clinically professional and that's how I like to work."

7055

DAVID WILSON HOMES

From here they are master-minding the transformation of an old RAF camp into a 2,000-house instant community called Chapelford Urban Village in Burtonwood. "The first bus service could be up and running by 2006."

I SOFT

They do software application systems for healthcare provider organisations, when a list in a diary used to work fine.

CABLE AND WIRELESS

This is a data centre for the firm that lost loads of money on doomed internet projects. They now pay an Italian Chief Executive £2 million a year to try to turn their fortunes around. Oh, that figure does include £184,145 to cover the cost of Francesco Caio commuting between Milan and London.

NORWEST HOLST

Pretty little building from where they devise some not so pretty structures. They're part of the Vinci group who are big on vast distribution sheds, not least for Prologis.

SECURITAS

It's a cinema that's closed down, we thought. As we poked our camera between the bars of the locked gate to take a snap, suddenly a shutter door started to roll up to reveal a Securicor vehicle that edged out into a compound, so the door could close before the gate opened. So there were people in there. We went to the anonymous metal door round the back and told a camera who we were. "People wouldn't be interested in this," said a voice on a loudspeaker. Apparently the vans come up by lift from a bunker below.

"CHRYSANTHEMUM COTTAGE"

This was a farm worker's cottage on the Southworth estate. It's still occupied by a retired farm worker who remembers the arrival of the M6, which cut up the estate. The old gentleman grows a beautiful range of flowers but has never chosen to exhibit them in competition, though he would undoubtedly do extremely well.

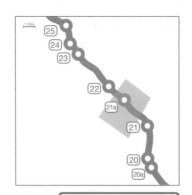

Manchester

What do you say in 100 words about a city that has so much energy?

Having come from the small calm of Newcastle-on-Tyne, the Editor remembers as a teenager the vibrancy of the place. He saw The Who at the Twisted Wheel nightclub in 1966. His first proper job was at A.E.I. in Trafford Park, as a computer operator on a machine that filled a big climate-controlled room and wouldn't do anything like as much as mobile phones can now do. His Dad helped build the Arndale Centre, and his Mum never got over the IRA blowing it up.

We'll return to Manchester when we tackle our book about the M62 next year.

ATOMIC ENERGY AUTHORITY (N.O.)

This 30 metre high grey shed was RD6, the place where boffins experimented with sodium rigs – very tall stainless steel vessels destined to be installed in Dounreay nuclear reactors. It's on the site of what was a massive high security complex for the UK nuclear power industry, which cooled down when the fast reactor programme was abandoned in the 90s. Security is now so low key that the Editor wandered round for half-an-hour trying to find someone to ask what the place was.

AIR MILES HOLIDAYS

UK HQ of the firm that delivers the travel arrangements (flights, hotels and car hire) for the 6.5 million people who collect vouchers from 100 organisations. You can see Pacific House, full of graduates of The AirMiles Academy.

ENVIRONMENT AGENCY

Their North West region covers 14,000 square kilometres occupied by 7 million people, who produce 24 million tonnes of waste. The Agency prevents pollution of water, land and air, regulates major industries and waste disposal, protects people and property from flooding, ensures efficient use of water and encourages conservation. They are most proud of cleaning up the Mersey to make it habitable for salmon and sea trout.

AMEC

A few years ago Len Fairclough (no, not the one from Coronation Street) was quite happy with a few building contracts, including some sections of the M6. But that wasn't enough and so, due to take-overs, amalgamations, foreign investments and the like, Len's now a little cog in this massive multi-national "engineering services" company, employing 45,000 people worldwide who pull in £4.7 billion each year.

They face compensation claims at the Manhattan Twin Towers and kidnap threats in Iraq.

Irlam

Why does this small, inconsequential Manchester suburb get an entry? Because it has a blue sign on the carriageway, of course. We drove through and found it very, well, inconsequential, apart from the Animals in Distress Sanctuary on Silver Street and design consultancy Morson Projects housed in a stylishly refurbished Co-op Wholesale Society building.

Leeds

The Editor's old mate, Phil Bishop (exceptionally able and amiable light entertainment multi-camera TV director) reckoned the only good thing about Leeds was the south-bound slip road on to the M1. Shame on him. We shall bring our objective journalistic skills to bear on the place in our next book, the M1 Sights Guide, starting soon.

WIDNES-MANCHESTER

When Simon and Garfunkel appeared together for the first time in 22 years on a British stage at the Manchester Arena in the summer of 2004, they revealed that Widnes Railway Station, which lies to the west along this line, was the inspiration for 'Homeward Bound'. A moment of silence, please.

Warrington

They've got the greatest town hall gates we've ever seen, and at Daresbury they boast one of the most powerful academic computers outside the United States. It's capable of doing all the maths homework and classwork of every child in Britain in – wait for it – one fifth of a second. It's called the HPCx, and is housed in the main lab of the government-funded Research Council. It's the ninth best supercomputer in the world and can knock off 3.5 trillion calculations a second.

WARRINGTON PARISH CHURCH

The church is quite a way off from what is now the middle of Warrington and is surrounded by a council housing estate and a supermarket. The spire was the highlight of major rebuilding work in the 1860s. It reaches 281 feet from the ground, making it the third tallest parish church spire in England. Within the church is the Percival vault containing the remains of a distinguished family of Warrington doctors, one of whom was the very first person to be enrolled in the new Warrington Academy of 1757, which helped get him in a book called 'Warrington Worthies', and now in here.

SAFEWAY

William Young in his "Sold Out – the true cost of supermarket shopping" tells us they were guilty of discriminating between suppliers over credit periods, instigated promotions on a product without the agreement of the supplier and requested the supplier retrospectively to fund the promotion, and expected suppliers to make a financial contribution to the cost of bar code changes or reduced-price-marked packs.

ALCAN RECYCLING PLANT

Since 1991 it has been making car body ingots out of aluminium drinks cans from all over Europe. Each ingot is made from 1.5 million cans, and the plant can turn out 70,000 tonnes of aluminium in a year – which is the equivalent of every aluminium drinks can sold in the UK. It's the biggest facility of its kind in Europe.

THELWALL VIADUCT

From this perspective, down on the Grappenhall - Statham road, you can see the twin official opening plaques, the first by Rt. Hon. Ernest Marples MP, Minister of Transport, on 29 July 1963. Engineer: James Drake CBE, County Surveyor and Bridgemaster, Lancashire CC; contractor: Leonard Fairclough. And, to the east (right), Thelwall New Viaduct, opened 25 July 1995 by John Watts, Minister for Railways and Roads; consulting engineer: Pell Frischmann; contractor: Tarmac. The original bridge was re-opened as the northbound carriageway on 23 December 1996.

BIRCHWOOD SHOPPING CENTRE

The blue chimney marks the air conditioning plant for this mall full of chain stores apart from St Rocco's Hospice shop, the Warrington Guardian 2003 Business of the Year. Last year the Hospice shops raised £350,000 for care and support for patients and their families with life threatening conditions, particularly cancer.

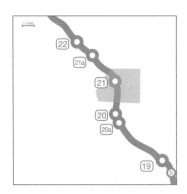

WOOLSTON NURSERY

Geoff Mawdsley's been here for 20 years, selling bedding plants – everything from Alyssum to Zinnia. He wishes the likes of Alan Titchmarsh would give him 12 months' notice of what they recommend because a TV endorsement can cause a surge of interest that can't be met for a whole growing season.

MOSS FARM

The Mawdsley family came from Southport at the invitation of Lord Warrington to cultivate this moss land many generations ago. Richard now produces red lettuce for London and cabbage for Manchester, but he's about to cut out the middle man by running a farm shop at Culcheth Garden Centre.

BROOKFIELD FARM

Michael, cousin of Richard next door, has 65 acres of horticulture on peat soil. He takes lettuce, cabbage, carrots, potatoes, onions and beetroot to London markets, keeping his fingers crossed for a good price.

BROWNMOOR COTTAGES

Is this the nearest occupied house to a motorway? One cottage is a mere 8 feet from the hard shoulder, which was being used as a carriageway through the whole of 2004. Eric Livermore has been renting and is now trying to buy his cottage despite the fact the building shakes in the night as every 40-tonner roars past his back door.

TRANSCO TANKS, PARTINGTON

These high pressure containers (like those at Bristol docks in our M5 book) contain domestic gas in cooled, liquid form. The site is surrounded by safety instructions: "No smoking... naked flames... danger, moving vehicles... protective equipment must... all activities subject to... no unauthorised... no admittance..." etc. We got there over the Ship Canal toll bridge, 12p one way.

RIVER MERSEY

Source NW is a quarterly free magazine produced by the Mersey Basin Campaign, which works towards better water quality and sustainable waterside regeneration for the rivers and waterways of the North West. The Summer 2004 edition points out that a bottle of Evian must travel over 750 petrol-guzzling miles until it lands on a supermarket shelf in the North West.

MANCHESTER SHIP CANAL

16,000 men laboured for seven years to remove 77 million tons of earth to create the 36-mile long "big ditch", which was officially opened by Queen Victoria at Salford Docks in 1894. During the 1950s and 60s the Port of Manchester saw 5,000 ships dock each year, carrying between them 16 million tons of cargo. As well as labour disputes and containerisation, some historians point to the establishment of the M6 as a causal factor in the decline in use of the Ship Canal.

J20

FIDDLERS FERRY POWER STATION

This proved one of the most difficult sights to find by car. Eventually we reached the Halton Tourist Office, where it was charmingly explained we were on the wrong side of the Runcorn bridge. The girl drew us a map, and suddenly we were less than a mile away, and able to park our car, buy an egg, cheese and mushroom bap from a catering van and walk close enough to get this picture – which doesn't do the place justice – because it is unquestionably the most impressive sight in this book.

Some staggering statistics: It uses 3,000 tonnes of coal an hour. The coal is pulverised into a powder and blasted into the furnaces. The coal comes from overseas and 100,000 tonnes are delivered by 20-wagon trains each week. That's 5 million tonnes a year. The turbine house is 263 metres across and 27 metres high, the cooling towers are 87 metres in diameter and 114 metres high, the chimney is 199 metres high. The cooling system draws 50 million gallons from the Mersey every day; it requires 85,000 litres per second. The four 500-megawatt turbo generators have the capacity to meet the combined peak power needs of both Liverpool and Manchester at any time.

M56

BP produced a little Book of British Motorways in 1975 – highly diagrammatic across long, thin pages showing the routing, junctions and signage for every carriageway. We think it's almost completely indecipherable. It devotes a page to the M56 from the A56 to the A560. Hard to imagine anyone finding it useful.

Runcorn

J20a

No one has ever waxed more lyrical on Cheshire than Arthur Mee, who describes it as the Romantic Gateway to the North: "a county of the dairy farmer, producing food for the great industrial areas which at many points have thrust their busy towns across her boundaries. Along the Manchester Ship Canal busy towns are expanding year by year, milling grain, refining oil, and doing a hundred things." Chances are he had Runcorn in mind.

CROWLEY HALL

Mrs Swift is a formidable farmer, evaluating commercial prospects forensically. She lost 300 cattle to foot and mouth 3 years ago, and now concentrates on potatoes for chips. The 1677 Hall has 120 acres. But she and her husband and sons farm 600 acres of neighbouring land as well. An acre will produce 20 tonnes of spuds. Agents determine the price, and it can be several disconcerting months before you see the money.

6946

LIVERPOOL AIRPORT

They've given it the name the John Lennon Airport, which sounds good. But no PR will ever shake off the stain of the car thieves who ran over a man about to go on holiday with his wife and were vulgarly scornful of the judge who sentenced them to a mere seven years for manslaughter.

6933

RADICAL POLICIES

"Almost without exception, the ecological implications to the planet of tourism based on air travel have been overlooked." "Although successive governments have had energy efficient policies for many years, and have pledged action on climate change, their more prominent objective continues to be to promote growth in the economy. Radical changes in government priorities are required to prevent serious climate change and we as voters have to press for and accept the changes that this entails." Mayer Hillman.

BRIDGEWATER CANAL

Francis Egerton, the third Duke of Bridgewater, cut a canal from his Worsley coalmine to Manchester, reducing the price of coal in the town by nearly half. This encouraged him to create a route from Manchester to the Mersey that opened in 1767 and even ran a passenger boat service.

Lymm

This is a sweet little place, with the Bridgewater Canal cutting along a contour, forcing roads to go over or under the waterway, all of which adds to its charm. And the post office does a sideline in carpets.

OUTRINGTON CHURCH

At the bottom of this steeple are two emotive memorials: "Baby Daniel, Born Asleep, 15th August 1999. There will always be a special place in our hearts for you. Love and miss you. Mummy, Daddy, Emma, Adam and Nana XXXXX."

"Our beloved daughters Lauren Elizabeth and Aimey Jane Donald, born asleep 28th October 1995. Until the day we meet again our love for you shines bright, our beautiful little angels, goodnight, god bless, sleep tight."

POPLAR 2000 SERVICES

This was Truck Stop of the Year 1997 and 1998. There's 21 acres of lorry parking with 4,000 trucks visiting on a typical weekday and up to 400 stopping overnight. It's all ruggedly utilitarian compared with normal motorway service areas. There's a noticeboard for the United Road Transport Union ("It's a long road ahead on your own") and a shop dedicated to CB radio and other trucker stuff. The cafeteria supper alternatives when we called on a Sunday night were steak and kidney pie and... eh, that's it.

Macclesfield

Two local farms, Messuage and Lima, have recently become beneficiaries of Defra's Countryside Stewardship Scheme, receiving payments to enhance and conserve landscapes, their wildlife and history, and to help people enjoy them. Messuage promises sightings of buzzards and skylarks, Lima guarantees exceptional views of the Peak District – subject to the weather, of course.

Tatton Park

This place is run by the council but they farm the gardening out to the National Trust, who are considered to be doing a great job. It hosts the Royal Horticultural Society's annual Northern Show, which, in the summer of 2004, displayed "Elevated Outdoor Living Spaces" – fancy designer tree houses erected in your back garden, subject to planning permission, alongside your tree, for £20,000.

GRASS DRYING PLANT (S.O.)

This was built 34 years ago by the father of the current farmer Alan Percival. It will dry all types of grasses in 7 minutes sucking the stuff through a big revolving heated drum after which steam rises out of a chimney and the dried grass is turned into cattle feed pellets. Since foot and mouth they've diversified into drying newspaper pulp from Ellesmere Port. Short fibres are dried and later ploughed into the land or used as cattle bedding. Lorry drivers warn each other about the "cloud factory" by CB radio. It has its own call sign.

Chester

The fourth edition of the Methuen Little Guide to Cheshire published in 1957 devotes five and a half pages to Chester Cathedral, then advises readers that "old houses are so numerous in Chester that a detailed description of even the most important would occupy too large a space in this little book."

Northwich

Cheshire has been an important source of salt for 2000 years, though the Celts were at it even before the Romans came along. And to this day it's providing 13,000 tonnes for the county's very own roads through winter. Find out more at the Salt Museum. In the summer of 2004, the Lion Salt Works was a candidate for the BBC's Restoration series. Shame Griff never has time to visit a hairdressers.

NEAR MISS

Closest the Editor has come to an accident on the motorway so far was when he had just come on to the carriageway here heading south after a visit to his parents for Christmas. There was snow on the ground, and a heavy snowstorm commenced just as he reached the motorway. Suddenly ahead of him about a dozen vehicles started to skid and slide into each other. It seemed inevitable he would slew into this multiple pile-up, but he managed to steer on to the hard shoulder and up on to the bank beyond it and sort of sledged past the chaos on the carriageway. He carried on, leaving the mess of pranged cars behind him and came off at junction 18 and edged home by trunk roads, his son, in the back, oblivious.

KNUTSFORD NORTH SERVICES

On the sunny morning of Sunday 1st August attractive female agents for GlaxoSmithKline were sighted dropping off 400 emergency bottles of Ribena and Lucozade to top up the supplies normally delivered through the week. We were amazed that this multi-national drugs giant saw fit to supplement its massive income with endeavours of this order.

CHESTER-MANCHESTER LINE

Ultimate destination eastward was once the fine Manchester Central Station, but that's now become the city's G-Mex Exhibition Centre. The city has the start of an impressive tram infra-structure and plans have been well advanced for its further development, but recently the government braked hard on supporting this promising public transport prospect.

BUCKLOW FARM

Peter Freeman handed over his farm work to his brother-in-law in order to pursue a career as a teacher. It must have been a good move because he's now the Head of a primary school in Widnes. In August 2004 he was concerned that the Highways Agency had not seen fit to send him details of the consultancy paperwork regards widening the carriageway which would obviously affect his house.

PEOVER GOLF CLUB

"It's Peever – not pee over" they were at pains to explain from the offices of their stylish oak beamed club house. The club only started in 1996, hence they don't have an entry so far in the Book of Cheshire Golf Clubs. Assuming you are approved, it costs £735 to join, after which you have to pay an annual subscription of £750.

TABLEY OLD HALL FARM

This glorious Gothic building is the icing on the cake of a redevelopment plan for the site which was part of the estate of the Leycesters of Tabley, who numbered in their family an historian, Sir Peter, author of "Antiquities of Great-Brettain" published in 1672. The Hall is now on the market for £5 million.

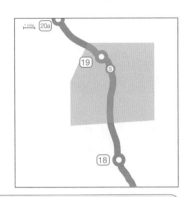

MANCHESTER AIRPORT

Apparently wealthy women from Dubai fly in each morning to go shopping at the John Lewis's at Cheadle Royal, then take the flight back home in the afternoon.

VALE FARM

Colin and Jill Sherwin have 100 dairy cattle on 100 acres, the milk going to Dairy Farmers of Great Britain. The farm has been in the family for three generations. Jill looks after 25 free range chickens and if you pass by this way you can buy some of the eggs.

KNUTSFORD SOUTH SERVICES

This has a scarily short ramp off the carriageway, so that if a newcomer determines to edge into an awkward parking bay near the entrance, a tail-back of cars can build rapidly back down on to the carriageway. However there is also an allocated dog walking stretch of grass, and water and biscuits available for dogs in the foyer, as is the case with all good Moto service areas. And pick up your Kennel Club ten point plan of Guidelines for road travel with your dog.

Knutsford

This is where the Cheshire set swan about in their SUVs (Sports Utility Vehicles). Apparently here one will find the greatest density of designer jeeps outside of Chelsea, closely followed by BMWs; statistically, that is, because as we know BMW drivers are congenitally fixated about accelerating past every other road user.
Often you can spot an SUV and a BMW on the same manicured drive, behind the automatic gates. Em, okay, we've just made all this up.

HUCKNALL FARM

Stephen is the third generation Jennings to run this dairy farm, their end product going to Express Dairies in Manchester. Another dairy farmer near here told us of the Tesco buyer who came out to visit a farm and was shocked to see cattle messing in the yard, and declared that the farm could no longer supply the supermarket because of these unsavoury conditions. The farmer had to explain to the buyer that this was normal, natural dairy cattle behaviour.

GOING SOUTH

Not many hitch-hikers in their late 60s, but Frank is an exceptional man. He's had a lifetime of casual work from restaurant management to motorway construction labouring, and now he can't settle. We picked him up at Knutsford services and took him as far as Hilton Park, and on the way he told us many stories of hitch-hiking rides he has had on the M6, including from women who work the lorry parks through the week before going home to their husbands at the weekend and Rolls Royce drivers en route to the Cheltenham races. Our favourite was the Irishman, unable to read, who picked up Frank to have the destination signs read aloud in order that he could get to Stratford-on-Avon.

VALE DEPOT

If you buy a Chinese takeaway, chances are it's got bean sprouts inside, and, if so, chances are they came from here.

An enterprising ex-Hong Kong businessman saw a gap in the foil container and so set up shop here to fill it.

Patently it depends on cheap fuel and easy access to the motorway system, plus a big shed for sorting.

SHAKERLEY MERE

This was a woodland until the Second World War, when the timber was felled for fuel. In the 1950s and 60s sand was extracted for coloured glass making, then woodland was reinstated around the big pond which offers daily fishing for 20 pound carp at £3. The Cheshire and Wirral Ornithological Society have started work on a bird atlas that will embrace this site.

BUCHAN

This is a concrete works servicing the insatiable needs of the giant construction outfit Amec. As a tiny subsidiary of the global civil engineers, they do a useful variety of pre-cast concrete products.

NEW FARM

When Patricia Davies's grandparents were ready to retire from farming they built a bungalow nearby to live in. A few years later the motorway came along, cutting them off from the family home. The old folk rejected the offer of a high fence or foliage, because they wanted to watch their family farming. Yes, that's the bungalow, directly opposite. It's now rented out at £500 a month.

RIVER DANE

This starts life in the Peak District and meanders through Cheshire's soft sand and gravels. The upper stretches are walkable, but that's not so easy around here. The Council's Walkers leaflet recommends starting at Brereton Heath Country Park and crossing the river to reach the village of Swettenham as the best way to enjoy the Valley.

Middlewich

"Ches (5,460) An ancient trading place modernized and busy extracting salt from its abundant brine springs. It lies near the River Dane and on the Trent and Mersey Canal. Church, St Michael and All Angels, is Gothic, with monuments and a brass of 1591. Near, in 1643, Lord Byron led the Royalists in a victorious battle over Parliamentarians." AA Road Book Gazetter 1936.

Cheshire

There cannot be many counties that work so hard to keep their citizens as well informed as the fortunate folk of Cheshire. Alsager Library was packed with intelligent, well-presented free literature explaining every aspect of the resources and policies being deployed, from Environment Reports to Structure Reviews, the Constabulary Corporate Plan to "Biking the Backroads" recommended routes.

PLUM TREE FARM

Valerie Booth has been running a riding school and livery stables here for 8 years. Children aged 5 can happily take up riding, but those who start later at 10 or 12 become as proficient almost as quickly. Kids stick with it more than adults, who have a tendency to give up after just a few lessons. They either decide it's not for them, or they reckon they've got the hang of it.

CHEVRONS

These first appeared on the M1 in Northamptonshire and immediately reduced tail-gating by 15% (Why wasn't it more?). They are at 40 metre intervals and reduce multiple vehicle accidents by 40%, injury accidents by 50%, and single vehicle accidents by nearly 90%.

WOODLANDS FARM

Mr Halman is a busy man growing lettuces. He was too busy to talk to us, but not so busy that he didn't have time to argue that his glasshouses were not visible from the carriageway and to then take us to the perimeter of his farm, where we demonstrated that motorway users had roughly six seconds to register his premises. He then admitted he never used that stretch of motorway, and told us we'd been lucky to catch him as he'd just broken off for a brew whilst mending a tractor, and, as we could see, he grew lettuces.

GAS PLANT

In 2004, local residents were fighting John Prescott's decision to overturn planning inspectors' conclusions that it was a bad idea by Scottish Power to seek to build a Gas Processing Plant in Byley on the site of nearby Cranage Airfield.

LOCATION SIGNS

"Em, I've broken down on the M6." "Whereabouts, Sir?" "Near... I'm on my way to Manchester Airport." "Are you travelling north or south, Sir?" "Em..."

The signs are an experiment to see if they improve communication between broken-down vehicles and emergency services. Traditionally people, who have stopped on the hard shoulder, walk to the nearest orange phone box to advise the police of their problem, but more people are now using mobile phones to alert the police, and then can't explain where they are. These signs, at 500 metre intervals, should make it quite clear.

JODRELL BANK

The Editor's first motorised transport was a Vespa scooter that allowed him to travel here from Manchester to see Sir Bernard Lovell introduce a lecture by Colonel Glen, the first American in space, in 1966. The big dish still has a role to play in space exploration.

RIVER CROCO

With a name like this it should be in Australia or South Africa, but instead it rises at Charity Farm near Congleton and dribbles west into the Trent and Mersey Canal at Middlewich near where the Romans established salt works. These days it's apparently popular with underage smokers from Holmes Chapel precinct.

CREWE-MANCHESTER MAIN LINE

The journey to and from Hereford and Stockport was made many times by the Editor to visit sickly relatives up north. To the west the track passes close to old salt workings, which are a permanent civil engineering problem requiring close monitoring and frequent shoring up.

Holmes Chapel

There were just 20 houses in this hamlet in 1753. Then on the morning of the 10th of July of that year, 18 of them burnt to the ground whilst the villagers were at Northwich Fair. By 2000 however the place ranked as 17th least deprived district in England according to government league tables on employment, health, education, housing and access to services.

Crewe

Churton's Railroad Book of England of 1851 (Historical, Topographical and Picturesque) told travellers that: "Crewe Station is a very handsome building in the Elizabethan style, and a great railway depot. The population is chiefly employed in the stations and foundries of the several railways which centre in this locality, to which circumstances Crewe owes its origin and prosperity. The town consists of very neat houses appropriate to the wants and comforts of the officers and servants of the railway companies."

Sandbach

The citizens used to be very proud of their Literary Institution designed by Sir George Scott in 1857 to "afford accommodation to the inhabitants of the town." Ramsay MacDonald once addressed a by-election rally in the library.

Our straw poll in the fish and chip shop indicates that these days locals don't know much about the Institute, except that a brass band rehearses downstairs and taekwondo classes are held upstairs.

SANDBACH SERVICES NORTH

When we arrived here the HM Customs and Excise Road Fuel Testing Unit were in the midst of a morning of examining every coach's diesel for evidence of rebated fuel – cheap kerosene or tractor diesel – being illicitly used by drivers. They had been at it for 4 hours and hadn't identified a single infringement.

TRENT AND MERSEY CANAL

The Editor took the canal boat his father had built for a cruise along here. At a lock to the east he was about to leap from the bank to the boat when his wife accidently drove the boat forward. So he fell into the water, losing his spectacles. Without them he was incapably shortsighted, so she set off to go home by train to get his other specs. She lost her handbag at Kidsgrove station, but managed to return a few days later with the spare specs. A year later police arrived at their house demanding fingerprints, shoe sizes and diaries. A month earlier Kidsgrove was the location of an incident relating to the kidnapping of coach heiress Lesley Whittle. The police had found the missing handbag in a toilet cistern of a pub near Kidsgrove station and in it was a Visa card in the Editor's name.

OAKHANGER AQUATICS

Ex-pig farmer Norman Evans has been selling exotic fish from here for 20 years. He has over 100 species in stock, from 1 inch long tetra to 24 inch koi. He offers lots of advice to newcomers, especially about letting tanks settle down before putting the fish in. Some people set up with inappropriate pet shop products and inadvertently create a deadly toxic environment.

CREWE-STOKE

We walked up on to the footbridge at Radway Green to get a shot of the old Ordnance factory, thinking we were at a small railway station. It turned out this was top secret access to the BAE systems car park. We continued to behave like train spotters and snapped this passing loco where once they used to load up freight wagons with armaments.

Stapeley Water Gardens

Outdoor clothing and children's fun wear, barbeques and chimineas, conservatories and sheds, Gold Macaws and Amazon Parrots, light bites and hearty meals. It's all built round aquatic accessories and an elaborate hot house that contains a frog that eats whole mice, and Suzie, 5 metres long and weighing 75 kilograms, who sounds capable of eating whole visitors.

6670

6638

ST JOHN THE EVANGELIST, SANDBACH HEATH

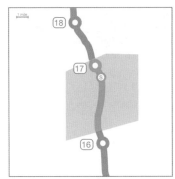

On the glass doors above the confetti a sign said: "It has come to the attention of the PCC that some people are visiting the churchyard with dogs and allowing them to do their mess in the churchyard, and on some occasions, on the graves. This is very unpleasant for those who maintain the churchyard and causes distress to those who loved one's graves are dirtied."

Congleton

They used to be big on boozing here. In the 18th century there were 40 common alehouses in the town. Then in the 19th century 100 beer shops opened around the alehouses. Landlords had to swear before magistrates they would not knowingly "suffer any gaming by Journeymen, Labourers, Servants or Apprentices" or permit any Bull, Bear or badger-baiting." Councillors once borrowed money from their bible fund to buy a bear for the annual fair.

SANDBACH SERVICES SOUTH

An Amey Mouchel Incident Support Unit on a tea break here told us they like dealing with Road Traffic Collisions most of all and picking up litter least of all. On the hard shoulder or beyond in recent months they had collected a sack of pigs' trotters, an old toilet and some live hens. Meanwhile the young man cleaning the exterior of the service area was in a state of shock, having just found a used syringe by a kerb.

LOCK CAFÉ

A host of canalside services here on the Cheshire Ring Walk. Next to Hassell Green Post Office is the café that becomes the 57 Brasserie at night. How about tomato fondue mousse with basil pesto dressing, tomato chutney and dressed leaves for starters?

Nantwich

As a radical alternative to the water gardens, Nantwich's other big attraction is Rod Siebert's amazing Secret Bunker Museum, full of artefacts of Britain's nuclear defence systems. The Editor tried to do justice to it in a film about civil defence for Pebble Mill but the acting editor, too young to remember the Cold War, hacked it into shallow trivia.

BAE SYSTEMS (S.O.)

This was a massive Royal Ordnance small arms factory set up in the Second World War against the wishes of most of the population of Alsager. In 1942 it was turning out 15 million rifle bullets and 1 million aircraft cannon shells a week.

Where we took our picture a sign reads: "Anyone here without permission will be arrested and prosecuted under the Explosives Act of 1875."

FLASH FARM

Stewart Lawton's family have been here for seven generations since 1780. It's owned by the Duchy of Lancaster, which means they occasionally get invited to Buckingham Palace garden parties. At the end of their drive is a signpost with lots of teddy bears taped to it, marking the death of a teenager in a road accident a couple of years ago. It's so striking, Mrs Lawton fears the memorial will one day cause another road accident.

Alton Towers

It's 14 miles as the crow flies from the motorway and half that again by car. Rumour has it school attendance officers patrol the place with photos of regular truants and a long-range digital camera. The place has made life a misery for Stephen and Suzanne Roper, who bought a house next to the grounds back in 1969 before the theme park took off and now suffer constant noise and traffic jams.

J16

DOMVILLES

The house dates from 1730. Jeff Oulton's 200- strong dairy herd provides milk for the Muller Yoghurt factory in Market Drayton. Son Mark runs a restaurant next door in The Lodge.

And Eileen Oulton has been doing bed and breakfasts for 20 years, which includes the option of sleeping in a converted pig sty.

Newcastle-under-Lyme

This town, to the north-west of Stoke, is very proud of its painters, some of whom worked as designers and illustrators in the potteries. The Borough Museum and Art Gallery celebrated 70 years of the Society of Staffordshire Artists in 2004, and mounted an exhibition of the work of Reginald Haggar, head teacher of the Burslem School of Art, a designer for Minton and author of books on ceramics.

The Potteries

There are 30 factory shops lying across a few square miles around Stoke-on-Trent, not just the local big names like Royal Doulton, Moorcroft, Royal Stafford, Spode and, of course, Wedgwood.

You can do factory tours and have a go at throwing or colouring pots. There are also several pottery museums, ranging from the traditional to the fun activity centre set up inside Burslem's old Town Hall - Ceramica.

HUNGERFORD HOUSE FARM

Philip Robinson's grandfather bought this place, which had been part of the Earl of Crewe's estate, in 1948. The family remember vividly the motorway construction work that created a dust bowl in the summer, despite the fact that some land was marshy. Digging machines frequently got bogged down and were abandoned and covered over by fill. Philip readily acknowledges he must lose more land to improve the M6, which is so busy along here.

6590

6560

RAILWAY BRIDGE

This concrete structure was created to support the line from Crewe to Stoke, leaving sufficient space below to accommodate the new motorway carriageway. Trains continued to use the track whilst the bridge was being put together underneath, replacing the previous smaller bridge in the valley. When it opened it was the longest single span concrete bridge in Europe.
It's now closed.

6527

KEELE SERVICES NORTH

Do you remember Bernard Levin? A forthright journalist from the Times in the 1970s, who got himself on to "That was the Week that Was" as an acerbic commentator. And on the strength of his status, rather than his looks, started dating a celebrated media character, Greek Arianna Stassinopoulos. Well, they were sitting at a table in here one Saturday

morning when my son knocked over his large cup of Coke casting sticky fizzy drink and ice cubes all over the great man's exquisite footwear. Bernard Levin died after a battle with Alzheimers in the summer of 2004.

JUNCTION 16

This takes you to and from the top end of the A500, which loops through Stoke and comes out at J15. So if someone says "Come off on to the A500", make sure you know which exit, unlike the Editor, who when first delivering M5 Sights Guides to THE (Total Home Entertainment distributors) near here, made several pathetic "I'm lost" calls from 10 miles south before finding the place and being overawed by pallet-loads of DVDs next to his humble box.

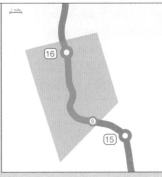

WEDGWOOD OBELISK

This stump is all that remains of a monument to John Wedgwood of Bignall End, Esquire, erected after his death in 1838. He was a lesser Wedgwood who got lucky by inheritance two generations on from the first commercially successful potters, Thomas and Josiah.

RED HILL FARM

Mandy Berrisford is a model ex-pupil of Rodborough College's Diversity course for farmers. They pointed her towards a gap in the market called koi. So she set up a business in one of her barns selling ornamental fish. The tiddlers are anaesthetised in Japan and flown over in a sealed metal flight case.

When she opens the box they look dead but come round after a few hours, as she nurses them in aerated spring water.

WALTON WOODS

The Forestry Commission manage this hillside that mixes Corsican pine and lodge pole pine with larch, willow, beech and sycamore. Planting and thinning out goes on constantly with most of the conifer timber going for fencing.

ETERNIT TILE WORKS

For Road Runner fans, Acme lives on. This factory is full of machines making Acme clay plain tiles from Etruria Marl. For those who fancy something fancier, they do decorative ridges, such as the slotted roll top with fleur-de-lys inserts, at the end of which you can have a falcon or dragon finial, i.e. a big clay bird or monster looking down from your roof.

ST JOHN THE BAPTIST, KEELE

This was built in 1870 for the benefit of the Sneyd family, most of whom are buried here. Thirteen generations of Sneyds occupied the Keele area, from William in the 15th century to Colonel Ralph who died in 1949. They got lucky in Victorian times when coal and iron were dug up on their estate and so they lived aristocratically for a while - hence Keele Hall, which now houses the University's swanky restaurants and senior common room. Lots of snaps of the Sneyds in the pub down the road.

KEELE SERVICES SOUTH

David Lawrence's glove compartment history of service areas, 'Always a Welcome', says: "it was believed that people were thrilled by the spectacle of speeding vehicles, and anything the (original) designers could do to bring customers into proximity with the road was encouraged".

O₂ have made a feature of their service cabin for their on-site mast.

Bridgemere

We suspect the new developers at Trentham Gardens have taken a leaf out of this place in terms of finding a commercial way forward. Old nurseries near Nantwich have blossomed into a big garden centre with a massive and distinctive range of plants, plus a Country Department Store, catering etc.

LYME FARM, BUTTERTON

Cyril Matthews is the fourth generation to farm here. He's got 160 dairy cattle and the same number of beef, plus 40 acres of maize. His grandfather took the place on in 1898 from a family that emigrated to Canada, where their offspring became big cheeses in the diplomatic corps. The next farm north (visible only while travelling south) is another Lyme Farm, once part of the Sneyd estate.

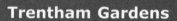

PARK MANOR

Highest point on the Butterton estate. During the First World War the 5th North Staffs regiment were billeted at Butterton Hall, now demolished. They all wrote their names on a wall before they went to the front. A lot of them never came back. The stables were home to wild Canadian mustang horses taken to the front to pull carts and guns.

Trentham Gardens

After years of neglect we are spending £100 million on regeneration, which will include a retail village - said the signs at the big building site at the edge of this 750 acre estate that was once home of the Sutherland family. 'Trentham Awakes' promises woodland and lakeside walks past historic gardens and amidst wonderful wildlife in "one of Staffordshire's best kept secrets." The Deer signs on the motorway warn of animals which have escaped from this "inspirational venue".

BEECH CLIFFE SAW MILL

Cousins James and Paul Forster saw up 100 year old oak trees from sustainable Worcestershire and Herefordshire woodlands here for beams and roof trusses, following in the footsteps of their grandfather Selwyn. If the traffic stops on the motorway, they go home to avoid the fumes. They like life "out of the fast lane."

STAFFORDSHIRE NORTH

Staff won a Staffordshire Newsletter "You're a Star" award: "For going the extra mile when acting as first aiders caught up in a traffic incident where the customer had suffered a heart attack and unfortunately died. Peter Bromley and Holly Rosbotham remained calm, professional and showed great compassion to the customer's companion, who was obviously in a state of shock."

The place was the 2004 national winner of the Loo of the Year Road Transport Category. But to use this facility you must travel for more than a mile on service area roads before you can re-join the motorway.

Eccleshall

This was briefly a key crossroads in the golden days of coach transport, sustaining eight inns, seven grocers, six maltsters, five tailors, four butchers and two clock-makers, according to the University of Keele Department of Adult Education, Local History Publication No 1. A road running into the town is known as Ghost Mile for sightings of a gentleman in Tudor clothes who had apparently hanged himself. Ecclians used to do a special dish to celebrate Mothering Sunday: roast veal and custard.

KEELE UNIVERSITY

When the Sneyds got down on their luck they hired out their estate as a holiday home to Grand Duke Michael of Russia from 1901 to 1910. He invited King Edward VII over and they got up to racing and racy stuff. Now the land is home to this relatively new university that has a hard-sell, sexy undergraduate brochure and futuristic office accommodation described as Innovation Centres.

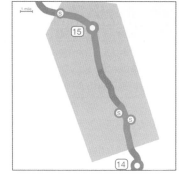

ROSE FARM

Not as nice as it sounds. The sour, burly proprietor snarled "Who are you and what do you want?" and things went downhill from there. He's a bitter man because of garden centres overgrowing his nursery business. So he now sells logs and sticks, plus space for advertising to motorway users. We didn't get a chance to tell him the Highways Agency plans to clamp down on such illicit hoardings.

JAMES IRLAM

As drivers leave the site, they face a notice that says: Keep your distance, Watch your speed, 20% of knocks happen at roundabouts, 25% of accidents happen whilst reversing, 30% of accidents happen at customer premises. Keep alert, do not take risks, only park in authorised areas and Be aware of your vertical height.

Stoke-on-Trent

Famous as the birth-place of the Wedgwoods and Robbie Williams. Sadly some of the Waterford Wedgwood work is now being moved to China. Yes, it's come full circle. In a national survey the city came out badly as regards doctor-patient ratio and air quality but good on commuter traffic speed. The football club recently hosted a national conference on terror attacks at sports venues. At the edge of the city is a retirement village, Berry Hill, home to 250 people aged 55 or over.

HOMESTEAD

One in a line of small-holdings houses built along a lane by Staffordshire Council in the early 1930s, this has long been occupied by Ernest Johnson, who struggles to earn a living from his suckler cows since the markets at Stone and Newcastle closed. He feeds them his potatoes and supplements his income by form book horse race betting. His new neighbours are not farmers. One erected a hedge that poisoned several cows. At 90 Ernest puts his longevity down to toast and black treacle for breakfast.

YARNFIELD YOBS

27 teenagers put this nearby village on the national map when Cannock magistrates applied Anti-Social Behaviour Orders to them for causing harassment, alarm or distress to people by hurling abuse, insults and missiles – the biggest court action of its kind to date.

STAFFORDSHIRE SOUTH

You wonder if Roadchef had an inkling that additional motorway lanes, or even a parallel toll motorway might be built along here because their Esso petrol station and Travel Inn lie well back from the carriageway. Even farther away is the stylish frontage of their main building with its glass, steel and water features to please the Wimpy consumers.

MILES

ROUTE CONSULTATION

In the summer of 2004, the Highways Agency launched their Management Strategy Public Consultation paperwork for Junctions 11a to 20 (from the M6 Toll to the M56), one of the busiest sections of motorway in Europe, 91 kilometres long. Key stages were: Collect and Analyse Data, Identify Route Problems and Issues, Hold Seminars and Workshops, Prepare Draft Strategy, Public Consultation (i.e. this bit), Review Strategy and Finalise Strategy. The pretty leaflet declares that the Strategy will address the following: noise, air quality, litter, drainage, biodiversity, landscaping, congestion, variable journey times, future traffic growth, restrictions to development, freight transfer opportunities, community severance, safety issues for pedestrians, cyclists or horse riders at junctions, emergency vehicle accesses, effects on local roads, queuing on slip roads, excessive speed, slip road safety, weaving, lighting, road spray, service areas, layby and service area security, and freight and investment initiatives, i.e. everything. But it doesn't actually tell you what the strategy is, apart from: "through better management it will reduce congestion, accidents and the adverse impact of the route on both the environment and local communities, and provide better facilities for motorists and freight." Then the Questionnaire asks: "Overall are you in favour of the strategy?" You had to go to the local libraries and ask for the Draft Document and find Para 6.3 on page 32 to discover the core notions: Widening to dual 4 lanes and tolling "for the longer term."

REST IN PEACE

Half way down the slip road off the northbound carriageway to Junction 14 is a small wooden cross marking the death of Saul Benjamin Harvey in a fatal motor accident here. Police Sergeant Steve Robinson has the arduous task of attending all the RTA (road traffic accident) fatalities on this stretch of the motorway when he's on duty. His advice to us motorway users is: Drive as safely as you can; keep your distance; reduce your speed; pay attention to what you are doing and to what others around you are doing. (Which are very good reasons for only reading this book at home!)

RIVER SOW

This rises near Market Drayton and runs through Stafford before joining the Trent. A couple of miles upstream it is joined by the Meece Brook, on which sits the National Trust-owned cottage of the celebrated and articulate angler Isaak Walton. Downstream from here is the Doxey nature reserve.

WORKS UNIT ONLY

This is the Doxey depot where the motorway maintenance team for the stretch from Junctions 12 to 15 are based. The contract is with Optima, a creation of Atkins and Jarvis.

The Department of Transport also run vehicle checks from here, escorting lorries off the motorway if they are suspected of being overloaded. And the Central Motorway Police Group have an outpost here.

NATURAL HIFTORY

In 1686 Robert Plot, Keeper of the Ashmolean Museum and Professor of Chymistry in the University of Oxford, published a study of Stafford-shire in which he noted: "the effects of an ill Clime upon Mens carriage and wits are not near fo deplorable as upon the Conftitutions of their bodies, which are not only alter'd but frequently deftroyed by it; fome of thefe Fenns and boggy places fending forth fuch contagious fmells... that the humors thereby if not abfolutely poifon'd, are at leaft incorrigibly diftempered, whence Scurvies, Coughs, Catarrhs &c Others produce a fort of Animals, fo fmall that they are invisible, and are fuckt in through the mouth and noftrils, which caufe grievous obftinate incurable difeafes."

STAFFORD GRAMMAR SCHOOL

This is a relatively new independent day school (private school) that was set up by a group of local parents who didn't like the idea of the old grammar schools being turned into comprehensives in the 1970s. The main building is a Victorian manor house designed by Augustus Pugin. There are two layers of glorified portakabins at the south end of the playing fields and the sports stadium at the north. They started with 17 pupils and 3 part-time teachers in 1982, and now have 357 pupils and 36 staff. Admission to the School is by examination, reference and interview. Fees in 2004 were £2,232 per term excluding meals but inclusive of text books and teaching materials.

WOLVERHAMPTON-STAFFORD

Wolverhampton was the scene of the longest and most bitter battle in railway history, described by Geoffrey Body as "a period of obstruction and attrition that is without parallel in the picturesque annals of railway rivalry." In 1850 Chief Constable Colonel Hogg and 50 constables plus a detachment from the 48th Regiment had to keep apart hundreds of rival railway workers building lengths of line for competing services.

MAY FARM

David Stubbs works from 5.30 in the morning til 8.30 at night seeing his 100 strong dairy herd produce 2,000 litres a day for the Midlands Co-op Society. His parents suffered the building of the motorway and he remembers big machines knocking their fencing down allowing animals to escape across the construction site. If the threatened carriageway widening goes ahead, he'll force himself to be philosophical.

IRON MOUNTAIN

It's a warehouse full of cardboard boxes full of office documents. This American company will eventually store 2 million boxes of old business files here, one of their 60+ premises in the UK.

Stone

A very old guide book to Staffordshire and Shropshire by Frederick Calvert explains how this place got its name: "Queen Ermenilda caused a church to be built over the stone tomb of her sons Wolfad and Rufin, who had been killed by their father Wulfere for being converts to Christianity. Afterwards Wulfere was converted and abolished idolatry from his dominions."

WEST COAST MAIN LINE

Stafford's a very important place railway-wise. This is where trains are heading north from the town towards Holyhead, Liverpool, Crewe, Stoke, Manchester and Glasgow. Railway infrastructure uses far less space than roads; a 10 metre wide railway track can carry the same number of passengers as the 135 metre wide motorway.

STAFFORD CASTLE (S.O.)

William the Conquerer first ordered a castle for "Stafford land" in 1070, but this was recorded as destroyed in the Domesday Book. Various Earls of Stafford built it up again and the place reached its heyday in 1575, when Queen Elizabeth the First came to supper. In the English Civil War Parliamentarians laid siege to the place, set fire to it and later demolished it. Around 1800, remnants of the Stafford barony built part of it again, but their offspring eventually abandoned it in the 1950s, after which it became a dangerous playground for local kids until one fell off the battlements and died in 1960.

THE KEEP

Here's how to look after a tower block properly.
It's run by Sanctuary Housing and has a good residents' association, a night time concierge, and a cheerful, hard-working maintenance man, Gordon Wilkinson, who diligently keeps the place tidy, and that includes removing the pigeons that have died from old age up on the roof.

Stafford

The M6 acts as a pretty effective by-pass for this town, which greatly benefits from being free of traffic through its centre. It's a pleasing place with the Guildhall accommodating an excellent art gallery, library, local studies centre and café. And the shopping's good with everything from a Co-op department store to an emporium selling battle dress. For the wheelchair-bound a custom-built Shopmobility office right by the Broad Street car park allows users to hire a wheelchair for £2. You can even call them on 01785 619456 from your mobile once you're in the car park, and they'll come to you. How about that for service!

ARGOS

The Editor's single experience is of standing in a line of glum people scribbling down digits from catalogue pages, queuing to give credit card details to surly staff before moving to another gloomy queue awaiting staff to emerge from the back with a shout and a box and an order number. They've got more than 500 stores selling more than £3 billion of stuff each year.

Shugborough

Lying north of Cannock Chase, to the east of Stafford, this is the home of the Earls of Lichfield (currently Patrick, photographer and second cousin to the Queen). It's owned by the National Trust and financed by Staffordshire Council. They put on all sorts of things through the year to keep visitor numbers up: Country Homes and Gardens Show, Spring Cleaning at the Farm, a Gamekeepers' Fair, bread-making, bonsai tree pruning, spinning and weaving, fireworks, open air theatre, boiling puddings, and washing and oiling pigs.

J13

ST LEONARD'S DUNSTON

A very fine, stylish and distinctive piece of stonemason's work marks the grave of George Edward Peter Baron Thorneycroft of Dunston, CH, PC. 26 July 1909 – 4 June 1994. The tomb, which has a parallel blank panel presumably awaiting details of his other half, is inscribed: "Enter not into judgement with thy servant o lord", and "Then we shall rise and see ourselves with clearer eyes in that calm region where no night can hide us from each others sight." He was Chancellor of the Exchequer under Macmillan from 1957 to 1958.

DUNSTON DAIRY FARM

This is a farm that's going places. They've recently installed a rotary parlour that revolves the cattle whilst they are being automatically milked. The animals move on to the constantly revolving metal turntable and have their clusters attached manually. It takes six minutes to revolve which is the milking time, then they come off and head back outside. There are 36 cows on the turntable at any one time, out of the dairy herd of over 400.

The big black drum we can see is something else: the 640,000 gallon capacity slurry tank that takes 6 months to fill.

6176

ST MICHAEL'S AND ALL ANGELS

Friends of the Church are vigorously soliciting support to sustain the place. Maintenance costs over £300 a day. To become an Ordinary Member of the Friends costs £10 a year. Or you can have life membership for £175. ("Please give more if you can."). When we visited, one man was doing his own thing – wheeling his lawn mower through the cemetery to attend to his late wife's grave. The wayside pulpit dayglo notice asks: Where will you spend eternity?

6128

PENKRIDGE

Horse and sheep fairs featuring loot from raiding parties into Wales caused this market town to prosper back in the 14th century. Today they still have stall markets creating traffic jams through the town on Wednesdays and Saturdays. The Civic Society have tarted up the Old Gaol into a Heritage Centre, manned by cheerful enthusiasts; a contrast with the local library staff who, when we called, seemed to sit on a spectrum between sullen and defiant.

J12

RODBOROUGH COLLEGE

South of Penkridge are the 200 hectares of "land based industries" training facilities. They do courses in Agriculture, Animal care, Countryside Management, Fishery and Equine Studies, Horticulture and Floristry. Plus a vast range of short courses including Keeping Chickens in your Garden (suitable for those with no experience).

JUNCTION 12

This takes the M6 over Watling Street (later better known as the A5) built by the Romans as a handy route from Dover to Holyhead (not that the ferries were running very regularly in those days).

HOLIDAY INN EXPRESS

On this site is also our old friend Tom Cobleigh with a pub called Catch Corner, and adjoining Wacky Warehouse. As a refreshing alternative, adults might like to try the Square Orange restaurant, a new venture by a local catering and pub company. Nice venue and appetising "fusion" menu. Only open six weeks when we called, the most popular dishes were salmon fillet wrapped in Parma-ham on a bed of spicy noodles, and the salmon, prawn and asparagus pasta.

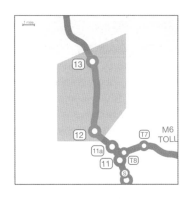

CANAL COTTAGE

This pretty private house was originally a canal worker's cottage. There was a pub next to it, which was knocked down in the 1950s. Underneath the cottage is a sluice system. On the towpath side is a rack and pinion device to allow a panel to open if the canal water level rose too high. The excess would pour underneath the house and spill out on to the field close to the carriageway. Staffordshire has more miles of canal than any other English county.

ST JAMES, ACTON TRUSSELL

TV shows were the theme of the 2004 summer flower festival. Displays across the church represented everything from 'Ready Steady Cook' to 'Bonanza'. 'Charlie's Angels' lay at the east window, 'Inspector Morse' occupying the vestry, and 'Wildlife on One' in front of the Vicar's seat. Unfortunately the organist was indisposed due to a broken pelvis, so Church Warden Delphine Howarth was advising visitors to sing heartily.

RIVER PENK

This rises north of Wolverhampton and flows north east into the Sow east of Stafford. The Romans established Pennocrucium at the crossing of the river in 48 AD as they advanced westward constructing Watling Street.

STAFFORDSHIRE & WORCESTERSHIRE CANAL

Considered one of the prettiest canals, it has been heavily criticised for failing to develop commercially in the face of looming railway competition. Charles Hadfield describes it as a prosperous canal in the 1840s occupying a key position "run by a group of apparently able men who could always spare a little money for the poor, or help build a church or school", yet subsequent to its opening in 1772 almost nothing was spent on improving its winding narrow line and single locks.

OTHERTON AIRFIELD

This was a Second World War relief airfield for the Pendeford RAF elementary flying training school (according to the Editor's father-in-law, John Featherstonhaugh, who trained pilots in the War). Now it's home to the Staffordshire Flying Club and Microlight Centre. How safe are microlights? "Only pilots suffering from a seriously diminished sense of self-preservation choose to fly outside the placarded limits." You can have a 20 minute trial for £40.

CANNOCK

This comms mast is 250 feet high and 4 miles away from the motorway at the nearest point opposite Penkridge. It's in the middle of Cannock Chase, an area of outstanding natural beauty and full of delights including the Birches Valley Forest Centre and a Museum. You can get a species recording card from the Wildlife Trust and hire a bike for the day. Near the base of the mast is Britain's German Military Cemetery, where the fallen of the two world wars were re-buried after the War Graves Treaty of 1959. Most of them were airmen, including the crew of four Zeppelins shot down in World War One.

Staffordshire

On some road signs designating the county it is described as "The Creative County". Who came up with this, we wanted to know? The Head of Tourism was on holiday when we called but his assistant explained that the slogan was created by the marketing department and adopted by the authority. It represents not just the creativity of the Wedgwoods, Dr Samuel Johnson and other creative people of the past, but current and future aspirations: creating advantage for industry and tourism, even creating white-knuckle rides at Alton Towers. Apart from the powerhouse of Stoke-on-Trent it's essentially a rural county with 2,000 hectares of Country Parks supervised by 19 Country Rangers.

The Editor remembers fondly directing the opening for an Antiques Roadshow from Biddulph, that combined images of abandoned coal mines north of Stoke with the beautiful gardens at Biddulph Grange.

"A FUTILE STICKING PLASTER"

In the summer of 2003, Transport Minister Alastair Darling announced a new £7 billion series of motorway and trunk road improvements, all of which were condemned by environmentalists. Eleven major measures mostly concerned widening existing motorways by a lane or two, and included linking the new M6 Toll motorway with the M54. Friends of the Earth described the raft of plans as: "a betrayal of Labour's pledges to improve public transport and not concrete over the countryside. The announcement is just a giant, expensive and futile sticking plaster applied to the running sore that is Britain's transport crisis."

The Green Party added: "This is the last nail in the coffin of Labour's pretensions to any kind of integrated transport policy. You can't make decisions like this in one breath and talk about tackling climate change in the next." A Guardian editorial considered: "If the government was serious about road congestion it would implement a sensible national motorway road pricing structure, rather than allow an under-utilised patchwork of toll roads."

J11a

FAST LANE

Toll users are made to feel good because they stay on the main carriageway and non-toll paying road users veer off to the left towards the old free M6. That's the case in both directions, and at either end when the free-riders re-join the main carriageway and link up again with those vehicles now a few pounds lighter.

In the first six months it was largely boycotted by commercial vehicles because of the high prices they had to pay (reflecting, say the toll operators, the damage these heavyweights do to the carriageway). But in July 2004 car prices rose and lorry prices dropped. Because of the lack of lorries, cars and police, the motorists using it were inclined to drive faster. Average speed on the Midlands Expressway over its first six months was 76 mph.

The head of Greater Manchester police traffic unit, Assistant Chief Constable Steve Thomas, was fined £450 and received six penalty points on his licence after being stopped doing more than 100 mph. A fatal accident on 30th July 2004 on the M6 near Walsall meant far more traffic took the Toll alternative which overwhelmed the pay booths to such a degree that the operaters decided to let some cars through free, simply because they were short of staff.

J11

HILTON PARK SERVICES NORTH

On the north side Top Rank built a projecting deck restaurant in 1967, but they didn't open it until 1970 because they reckoned there wasn't sufficient passing trade. It's now a white elephant again, with all the Moto action confined to the ground floor. This includes a Ladbrokes branch where you can bet on all sorts of things including greyhounds - if you can understand the Virtula Quickslip: "Combination tricast. Predict three or more greyhounds to finish first, second or third in any order. Place an 'x' or a '/' in the 1st box for each of your chosen Trap numbers, then place an 'x' or a '/' in the appropriate box to select your stake. If you pick 3 Traps the total bets are 6. For further assistance please ask us."

Telford

This new town is even more pleased with itself than old Wolverhampton. It's because the Borough of Telford and Wrekin came out as one of the top 10% best managed local authorities in England, according to the Audit Commission's Comprehensive Performance Assessment. It is the first authority to gain "excellent" marks in the West Midlands. The patch includes Ironbridge, where many consider the industrial revolution really got underway. Our recollections include a strange animation company that demanded visitors sign a secrecy agreement before entering the premises, because they were worried that someone might remember the look of one of the gruesome creatures on the electronic drawing boards and steal off and make a fortune from it.

J10a

KIT PAC BUILDINGS

You know those big nondescript industrial sheds that are all over the place? Well, this is where a lot of them come from, because it's HQ of the firm that produces folded modular buildings in corrugated plastic coated cladding. A patented British invention manufactured in the UK. They can be erected in days, even on bad ground, and can be even relocated if necessary.

SANDY ACRE

This scrappy place is home to a low-key animal feed business. They do stuff for horses, pets and pigeons. Apparently pigeons thrive on tic beans, which are grown here. Pigeon fanciers are highly sensitive about their birds. They live in constant fear of the creatures consuming inappropriate food, and equally menacing are the growing numbers of predator birds – wild hawks or raptors - which the RSPB vigorously defend.

FOR THOSE TAKING THE TOLL ROUTE YOU WILL FIND THE RELEVANT SIGHTS ON OUR PAGES 87-93.

M6 TOLL

This is one of the country's biggest recent road-building projects, costing £485 million. It's 27 miles long with 50 bridges, three maintenance areas and a new canal lock. It's owned by the Australian Macquarie Infrastructure Group who have admitted that the business is effectively a monopoly as there is no government control over prices, thanks to a contract drawn up under the Conservatives in the 1980s.

It was opened by Transport Secretary Alastair Darling on Tuesday 9th December 2003.

The bridge across the feeder roads just north of the line of pylons was extended to accommodate the new lanes. Apparently the concrete first used was too soft, so they had to knock it down and start again at an extra cost of around £1m.

HILTON PARK SERVICES SOUTH

There's a Travelodge here, which is not terribly remarkable as they don't half get about. Look at the handy map in the back of the Directory and you will discover that they are so thickly dotted across England not much remains unLodged, except for a few sparse patches of Yorkshire, Northumberland and Cornwall.

The police have an office here that's seldom manned and mostly used as a rendezvous point and rest room. PC Nicola Hughes told us one distressing local problem is swans mistaking the carriageway for water and trying to land. She recently encountered a car on the hard shoulder with a broken windscreen and a dazed driver who had hit a swan as it took off.

M54

This runs westward to just beyond Telford before joining the A5 Roman road that continues to Shrewsbury and the A49, a busy trunk road running due south to Hereford.

TRUANTS

Near here a postal sorting man on sick leave with sciatica, walking his large Japanese hunting dog (like a fat, furry Alsatian) expressed his anger about kids illicitly out of school shooting wildlife with air rifles, lighting fires and throwing empty beer cans and cigarette packets all over the place.

NEW INVENTION

This vicinity is called "New Invention", but no one knows why it got that name. Various theories are put forward; one that it had something to do with the creation of a new type of lock and key, which was an important local industry, another that it indicated a new seam of coal had been found in this area.

The local Primary School has a history of pioneering endeavours. The log book of 1941 explains that the timetable was modified for a week to try out 'Ann Driver's Music and Movement Lessons' broadcast by the BBC.

WYRLEY AND ESSINGTON CANAL

Prime Minister William Pitt personally backed the 1792 Act of Parliament that permitted the creation of this waterway designed to run from Wolverhampton to the coal mines of Great Wyrley (where the main northbound toll pavilion lies on the M6 Toll), but just a few years later the Birmingham Canal Navigation opened their Walsall Canal, effectively undermining the value of this route. Much of the Wyrley and Essington was a contour canal, which meant its path wandered through fields to stay on one level, hence it became known as the Curly Wyrley. It's the highest Black Country canal above sea level reaching 533 feet. This created a problem over water supply, the only sources being a tiny stream and water pumped up from the coal mines. The company built a big reservoir at Chasewater but this collapsed, flooding nearby fields, ruining farmland and drowning livestock in 1799. It was taken over by the BCN in 1846. The last coal boat made its final journey in 1968. If the utility companies can't cut a channel underneath a canal, then they sometimes have to stick a structure over the top like this one here.

Wolverhampton

The council is chuffed to have achieved city status in the year 2000, and is now on a recruiting drive: "Truly a City for the Millennium – vibrant, dynamic, forward-thinking and constantly improving. We've already come a long way. But now we're shifting up a gear. We're at the next stage of an innovative modernisation programme that will bring us right up to speed and maximise performance." That means their next Chief Officer of Commissioning, Contracting, Performance and Quality will be paid £70,000 a year. Howard Jacobson worked at the Poly for a while and lampooned it subsequently. The Editor did a post-grad Cert. Ed. for Further Education here and could see what Howard was getting at. He couldn't stop giggling.

AQUALUX

In here they make all sorts of self-contained shower enclosures from the simple varieties to the incredibly elaborate. At one end there are two glass doors cornered over a sealed tray that sits in a tiled corner of a room. At the other extreme two of you can share the 1420mm steam cabin with 12 chrome body jets, 2 foot jets, multi-functional shower head, light, mirror, radio, telephone and venting fan.

SHOWCASE CINEMA

To apply for a job here you must, of course, fill in an application form and attach a passport size photo. Amongst the questions are: Have you ever been convicted of a criminal offence? Have you ever been responsible for handling large sums of money? Have you ever been bonded? Have you ever been refused a bond?

Then you have to sign a statement that reads: "I hereby authorise you to conduct a full investigation of my personal, educational and employment history through the use of whatever investigative agencies or bureaus you may choose."

GROSVENOR CASINO

This contains Britain's biggest card room with 17 tables that can accommodate up to 200 players. They come from all over the world to participate in tournaments. One individual went away with £170,000 in poker winnings. Dozens of gambling premises regulations are neatly tucked beneath a stainless steel flap on the wall in the foyer, near lots of instructions leaflets and a self help guide for problem gamblers: "The following questions have been devised for gamblers to ask themselves: Have you put at risk important or significant relationships, educational studies, a job or your career because of gambling?" The manager told us people spot the place and come off the motorway at junctions 9 or 10 to track it down, only to discover 24 hours must pass before they can be permitted to enter.

JAMES BRIDGE HOLDER SITE GAS TANKS

Both these spiral guided tanks have the capacity to hold 6 million cubic feet of gas, which is about 170,000 cubic metres. They were built between 1956 and 1958. The James Bridge area has been the site of industrial enterprise for 500 years.

BALL & LEADBETTER HOUSE

Hopefully these will soon not be a sight. They are in a terrible state, and due to be demolished, though some elderly residents who have been here 40 years don't want to move. We got a guided tour from a single parent who has a great view of Birmingham from her balcony. But the lifts and landings are grimly vandalised and thus sub-utilitarian.

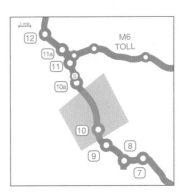

MAZAK

This is Bloxwich's old spelter works where they produce zinc alloy. Retired steel worker Les Cooper told us he remembers when the area was full of pools of water where limestone had been dug out. An old fellow ran a business collecting old engine oil and turning it into creosote for fencing. He cut tin boats from oil cans and let kids use them for a penny a go on one pond. One boy fancied a swim and made trunks out of a brown paper sack, but these disintegrated when the lad stepped out of the water.

SOUTH STAFFORDSHIRE WATER

HQ of company formed in 1853 supplying water to 1.25 million people over 1,500 square kilometres. Their website delivers a minute of black and white moving pictures of the Queen Mother opening Blithfield Reservoir in 1953.

THE VILLAGE

Fifteenth location for De Vere hotels, who are spending £16 million on 125 rooms here. Walsall hopes to get a "budget" hotel built nearby.

Walsall

King Henry VIII granted the manor of Walsall to John Dudley, Duke of Northumberland, whom Queen Mary had beheaded for treason. Dudley's servant, John Cocke, the Lancaster Herald, persuaded the Queen to allow him to bury his old master's head along with his body in the Tower of London. The Queen then sold Walsall for £1,000 to Richard Wildbraham of Cheshire.

Coal, ironstone and limestone were first mined early in the 19th century, and in Victorian times the town had 13 blast furnaces, 39 collieries and 250 saddlery workshops. Accidents were frequent: 22 miners died of starvation after a colliery flood in 1872 and 16 men were seriously injured when a blast furnace exploded in 1875.

Walsall was the first authority that ensured every primary school pupil was given a portion of fruit every day.

WALSALL CANAL

This was cut in 1799. A century later the Birmingham system of canals consisted of 159 miles, mostly on three levels: the highest around Wolverhampton, 54 miles at 473 feet above sea level; the middle around Birmingham 33 miles at 453 feet, and the lowest around Walsall, 20 miles at 408 feet. Thomas Pearce's 1813 Walsall Directory points out that "boats load at the wharf at the top of Park Street, every Wednesday, for all parts of the Kingdom."

AIR QUALITY ACTION AREA

The 1995 Environment Act obliges councils to monitor air quality. Walsall officers have discovered five areas where government quality targets will not be met. One is here around Pleck. There's too much nitrogen dioxide, mostly caused by exhaust fumes. Not surprising, as this is the busiest stretch of motorway in Europe. And the problem is aggravated by the prevailing winds pulling more muck in this direction from the Black Country. The council is supposed to discuss ways of improving the problem with residents, but a local environmental officer confided to us that there was not a great deal that could be done. Real-time air pollution monitors update the situation every 15 minutes. Apparently smooth driving lessens the problem marginally. Braking and accelerating churn out more fumes.

IKEA

Gillis Lundgren was a young Swedish draughtsman working for a furniture firm, trying to get a table into the boot of a car. He realised that the legs would have to be taken off, and so, one day in 1956, the concept of flatpack furniture was born. The furniture dealer, Ingvar Kamprad, has now become one of the richest men in the world with 186 stores in 31 countries generating annual sales of over £7 billion. According to Kamprad, "Happiness is not reaching your goal. Happiness is being on the way."

B&Q

They reported half-year pre-tax profits up 27% to £346m in July 2004, despite the wet summer having hit garden furniture sales. Kitchen, bathroom and bedroom business was up. Chief Executive Gerry Murphy said: "People consume their homes now". The controlling Kingfisher Group plan to spend £500m a year on new and refurbished stores this year and next. A government projection reckons there'll be 3.5m additional households in Britain by 2050. DIY for the foreseeable future.

CURRYS

Part of the Dixon group plc, the UK's biggest electrical retailer, despite having recently closed 100 of their High Street Dixons stores, which accounted for one third of their in-town premises. Annual profits before tax are in excess of £100 million.

WATERWORKS

You can see the chimney of this mid-Victorian pumping station for what was the South Staffordshire Water Board. Now it's home to the Brunswick Garage, and, next door, the Elite Gym for Men, which has a claim to fame in the impressive form of British powerlifting champion Dennis Dod, who trains on site.

ST. PAULS, WEDNESBURY

This church was erected and endowed by Edward, Henry, Alfred and Frederick Elwell in 1874. The family ran a garden tools factory that was absorbed into the Spear and Jackson empire. One of the brothers, Henry, left spade-making to take on the role of vicar from 1901 to 1906.

The current vicar, Jill Warren, reports in the Parish News that the new Bishop of Lichfield considers that: "Our children and grandchildren are bored by church and are not coming. We need to hand on our faith or the Church will die. And that will have a devastating effect on our nation."

BIRMINGHAM-WALSALL

There's a service roughly every half-hour through the day which stops at Bescot Station north of the Depot before going under the motorway en route to Walsall (some continuing to Stafford). According to Railwatch, Bescot is recognised as a hot spot for trespass and vandalism. On notices nearby they point out that 122 people died last year as a result of trespass and 11,500 hours of train delays were due to obstructions. If you see vandalism on railway property you should call the British Transport Police on 0800 405040.

BESCOT MARSHALLING YARD

This began life as a steam shed for the London North Western Railway in 1892, housing 32 locomotives. The diesel Traction Maintenance Depot opened in 1960. English Welsh and Scottish Railways is the freight bit of what was British Railways. EWS recently lost all Royal Mail work, which was a serious blow to its annual income. In the last five years they have managed to pull 34 million lorry journeys off the motorways, but the Chief Executive recently resigned due to frustrations over government's lack of subsidy for rail freight services.

PLECK FLATS

There are five blocks, 3 at 16 stories and 2 at 11, but they may not all be here next year as Walsall Housing Group is currently consulting with the residents as to whether or not some of these towers should be replaced with more conventional housing. There's a pretty little children's park in the middle, and a pretty awful portakabin across the Old Pleck Road where tenants can pay their rent.

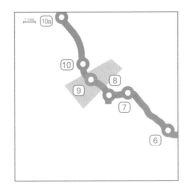

JUNCTION 9

In the summer of 2004, work commenced on carriageway improvement along here. One of the repercussions was to close the southbound feeder from junction 9. Instead, vehicles wanting to travel south on the M6 were directed to take the M6 north, with a view to turning round at Junction 10 and heading south from there. Unsurprisingly the southbound carriageway was quickly overwhelmed and so drivers would take other exits off junction 10 in search of a route south, so that the whole of the Walsall - Great Barr vicinity was soon near to grid-lock. The Black Country Business Chamber reckons that in a normal year millions of pounds are lost by local businesses because of delays to products and people.

BESCOT STADIUM

Taking every opportunity to provide and sell advertising space is the Saddler's ground, where Walsall play in the CocaCola League 1. Nearest to us is the William Sharp stand with a capacity of 1,900 for away fans. The experience on these terraces is described as "not perfect" by a web stadium directory. "No restricted view tickets are sold, so it's pot luck as to whether you are sat behind" a stanchion.

On the walkway from Bescot Station to the ground beneath the motorway are paving stones etched with poetry: "Deep peace of the running wave and flowing air to you. Deep peace of the quiet earth and shining stars to you."

MIDDLETON PAPER

Leonard and Sylvia Middleton opened a fish and chip shop in Darlaston in 1959 and soon found they were short of paper to wrap the food, so they started making it and selling it, which initiated a big new business purchasing rolls of paper from mills and converting them to sheets or reels. The typical roll comes in at 1.5 tonnes. The cylinder of fine quality paper is 1.25 metres in diameter and 1.5 metres in depth. If you unrolled it from here south-eastward along the carriageway it would reach to Fort Dunlop 20 kilometres away.

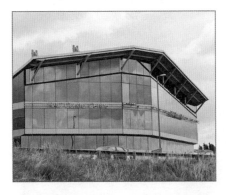

RAC

This is one of three national control centres for the RAC – which is a brand, and "no longer stands for the Royal Automobile Club." The motoring organisation attends to two and a half million breakdowns each year. This is HQ for RAC Roadside where 800 staff train and manage 1,500 patrol vehicles.

CORUS

Firsteel Coated Strip is the stuff that becomes non-stick baking trays. The blue chimney is an old gas scrubber that was used for cleaning drying oven exhaust but has now been supplanted by an environmentally friendly incinerator that burns the solvent fumes given off when lacquer or paint is bonded to metal at high temperatures.

ALFRED STANLEY & SONS

First produced horse harnesses and decorative clothing buckles in1856. They still make leather-covered buckles for Aquascutum coats, plus plastic versions for Clarks and K shoes. They devised the plastic-headed pins used for marking maps during World War Two, and so number Winston Churchill amongst their customers. These days it's plastic injection moulding and zinc alloy pressure die-casting.

F.H.TOMKINS BUCKLE

You've never seen so many buckles. They are one of Europe's largest manufacturers of pressed buckles; a Ministry of Defence approved supplier.

FRIAR PARK MILLENNIUM CENTRE

The light cream building up the road from UK Platforms is the sports hall for this community centre considerably enhanced thanks to lottery money. The hall hosts five-a-side teams and football training. Also on the site are health clinics, housing repair services, pensioner groups and youth clubs. Before the building of the St Francis of Assisi church, parish services were conducted in a wooden hut here.

UK PLATFORMS

From a distance the looming lines of these machines look like wacky lighting gantries for a small sports stadium. It's one of 15 national depots for a firm that hires out scissor lifts and boom lifts to provide access to high structures. The tallest scissor lift will take you up 18 metres, the highest boom will reach 38 metres. Amongst their customers are TV outside broadcast units covering sport, and Buckingham Palace maintenance crews.

ST FRANCIS OF ASSISI

This is the Parish Church of the Friar Park estate, built in the 1930s thanks to a generous endowment. In a neighbourhood that Father Peter Green describes as one of high deprivation is a spectacular Italian-style place of worship. Italian craftsmen were working on the sophisticated interior in 1940 when they were arrested as aliens and held captive until the end of the Second World War.

If you walk up to the building and try the door handle, you will see that the camera on the top of the tall steel pillar across the road follows your every move.

J8

CAMBERLEY & BRIARLEY

Camberley has 14 floors and 142 flats, Briarley 20 and 80, all privately owned. There was a third block, Marshall House, demolished recently to be replaced with "executive homes". Contractors used a 1.5 tonne iron ball on the end of a crane to break down Marshall House, but it kept bouncing off because the concrete was so solid. Caretaker John Wallis can't wait to retire as he's so sick of residents' stupid requests such as needing plasters for a cut toe every day for a week and borrowing plastic bags to go shopping.

M5

Most entries in this guide to the M6 get no more than 100 words. But with the M5 you have the option of another 40,000, by investing in a copy of our first book. We were mocked in some quarters for devoting so much time, space and industry to a motorway running from West Bromwich to Exeter, but it turned out we were not alone in being intrigued by the character and landscape of that route.

In the wake of the first wave of publicity, BBC Breakfast Time wanted to interview the Editor about the title, but he was convinced they intended to jeer at an anorak, so he turned them down. However he *diligently did other less high profile interviews, and posed for lots of photographs on motorway bridges.*

Three months later though, things looked different. He was now a relatively successful travel writer with plenty of sales under his belt. The second wave of publicity, which stemmed from a single article in the Birmingham City Living free listings magazine, led to eight live broadcast interviews on Good Friday, following up full pages articles in the Daily Mail and Times newspapers that morning.

But despite all that exposure, most people don't know about the Guide, and of those that do and use the M5, most don't buy a copy. Doh!

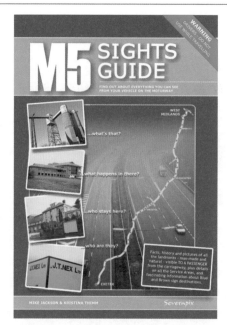

TAYLOR MADE

You're looking at the UK's largest indoor conservatory showroom with 20 fully built models to give you "a real feel for sizes, styles and colours". They have "no need for typical door to door sales people or telephone canvassers. All of our business is gained through customer recommendations and the use of high profile advertising to show our fixed price offers." Beaming out of their brochure is comedian and some time East Enders actor Mike Reid, who is "proud to be associated with a great local company." The "on-site manufacturing facility" turns out 50 units a week.

BUSTLEHOLM SUB-STATION

There's a buzzy, crackly feel in the air around here. Bear in mind that you are just whizzing – or, more likely round here, chugging – past it, but others have to live with it as it sits remarkably close to a large housing estate.

HOLLY COURT & OAK COURT

These are the last two tower blocks on the Yew Tree estate. 11 have been demolished to be happily replaced with conventional housing. Kenny Downing and "The Skull" from Judas Priest used to live nearby. At the heart of Yew Tree is the cheerful Healthy Living Centre where, if you want to find out how many calories you are burning each time you go for a walk, you can take one of their pedometers for a test drive.

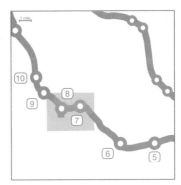

TAME VALLEY CANAL

Part of the Birmingham Canal Navigation system (about which every television programme that visits the city points out "there are more miles of canal here than in Venice") joining the Walsall Canal to the Birmingham-Fazeley and Birmingham-Warwick canals at Salford junction underneath Spaghetti Junction. This is the northern end of a loop under the motorway.

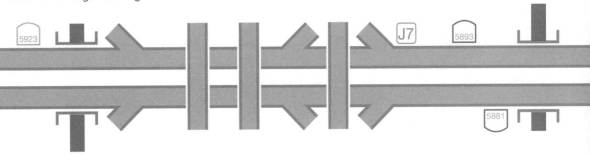

JUNCTION 8

The Ray Hall sewage treatment works that serves Dudley lies in the triangle demarcated by the connecting roads between the top of the M5 and the curve in the M6 which swings the motorway off its trajectory from the East to the West Midlands and routes it north towards the Lake District.
And so here is where the layout of our book changes from north-south to west-east.

RUSHALL CANAL

An 1847 addition to the 1844 Tame Valley Canal to ease access to the valuable Cannock coal mines further north. Guides for users warn of the smell of the Ray Hall works. This isn't half as bad as it used to be. In the 1960s the Black Country Trunk Sewer was installed, 14 feet in diameter and 20 miles long, to shift the waste of 2 million Midlanders to treatment works east of Birmingham.

PERRY BARR MOTORWAY FACILITY

Access roads left and right, up and down, show where maintenance and police vehicles reach and leave the carriageway to and from their buildings sitting under the motorway in the middle of a housing estate.

This is where the Central Motorway Police Group (page 81) is based, monitoring the Midlands network that runs from Staffordshire down to Worcestershire.

West Bromwich

"The Birmingham and Wolverhampton turnpike passes through this populous parish, and is one of the busiest and best roads in England. Sixty years ago there were only eight houses between Great Bridge and the Bull's Head, a distance of two miles, which now forms one continued street, with many neat villas, good houses, inns, and well stocked shops, giving the air and bustle of a market town." So said the 1851 Gazetteer of Staffordshire. West Brom now accommodates Britain's 9th biggest building society and, of course, the Baggies, back in the Premiership. And next year Europe's largest community arts development, "the public", will open here. You will be able to "realise your creativity in our exciting hands-on arts space". The town is part of Sandwell Borough, which proclaims to have demolished more of its residential tower blocks than any other local authority.

SUTTON COLDFIELD COLLEGE GREAT BARR CAMPUS

Down behind this fence is where the Editor first found employment in the West Midlands. He came from finishing his degree in Politics and Economics in Nottingham to be Assistant Lecturer in Liberal Studies here – teaching apprentice mastic asphalters about anything other than tarmac. He did one academic year at what was called Brooklyn Tech then left to become an advertising copywriter. Some of his students contributed to the fabric of the M6.

ROY FABRICATION

They make components for fork lift trucks and customise them if the masts are too tall for particular warehouse and factory doorways. They also produce a machine for removing the heavy batteries from fork lift trucks without manually lifting. It costs £30,000 and they sell 6 a year.

BIRMINGHAM CITY CEMETERY

Birmingham Corporation bought these 105 acres from Mr Wyrley Birch in 1859 for £15,750 to establish a new cemetery for the city. It was designed by Richard Ashwell of Coventry and consecrated by the Bishop of Worcester in 1863. A network of curved drives and straight avenues formed a handy cycle track for local youths when we visited. The Cadbury family are buried here, along with 600,000 other people. They do about 800 burials a year and reckon there's space for about another 4,000.

CHAMBER & COOK

This freight firm operates from an awkward site. A small loop of one-way narrow road has to accommodate all their vehicles that won't fit on their compound. Life got worse in the summer of 2004 when the Highways Agency shut off one of their access roads in order to repair the M6 from underneath.

KNOWLES AND CO.

Bill Knowles was a coal miner in the 1920s who got fed up walking five miles to the pit each day, so he bought a hand-cart and filled it up with sawdust from a sawmill and sold the stuff in the jewellery quarter for polishing purposes. He then started to supply engineering firms including Lucas and British Leyland who used the sawdust to mop up oil. Bill's stepson started trading in bundles of firewood, and now the next generation handle all sorts of timber products from partitioning panels to hardwood mouldings. Some years ago there was a brief fad for wooden skateboards and they managed to turn out 30,000 a week for 9 months.

5846

5870   5843

RA SERVICE ENGINEERS

They produce industrial storage systems for warehouses, and store their own stuff at the back of a container site behind their notice board.

AAH PHARMACEUTICALS

This highly-automated warehouse prepares twice-daily deliveries of 16,000 different products for hospital pharmacies and high street chemists.

CORPORATE EXPRESS

According to their website, they are the world's largest provider of office products. We left phone messages with several site and marketing managers on several occasions but they were obviously all too busy to return our calls.

Thankfully the helpful security guard let us have a copy of a recent edition of their European and Australian newsletter which had as a front page story the fact that, during the December 2003 Managing Directors' meeting, Italy was honoured for giving the best budget presentation.

THE HUB

This site began life as the 4-acre Kynock munitions factory in 1862. The office building dates from 1904. It became part of ICI in 1918 and helped develop the atomic bomb in the 40s and titanium in the 50s. In 1962 it became Imperial Metal Industries, IMI. In the 80s parts of the now 220 acre site started to be sold off for redevelopment.

SPAGHETTI JUNCTION

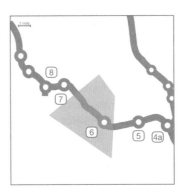

The Editor remembers the construction of the pillars for this monster as he took his bus journey from Erdington into the city.

The design was by Sir Owen Williams and Partners and the contracting work was undertaken by A Monk and Co from Warrington.

It cost £10m and was unique as Europe's largest and Britain's first free flowing interchange connecting the M6 with the Aston Expressway and local roads without reliance on roundabouts or traffic lights.

BIRMINGHAM-SUTTON COLDFIELD LINE

This suburban service began back in 1862 and was extended to Lichfield in 1884. In 1955, a York - Bristol express was diverted along here and passed through a 30 mph speed limit at 55, coming off the tracks at Sutton Coldfield and killing 17 passengers.

INNOVATE

The giant blue shed is stuffed full of chocolate. 75 bays shift 340,000 pallets a year all piled high with Cadbury Trebor Bassett confectionery, moved round the country by a logistics company called Innovate.

ASTON VILLA

"Aston Villa were founded in 1874 and by the time they became founder members of the football league in 1888, they had already won the FA Cup. The club moved to their Villa Park home in 1897. On the 26th May 1982 they defeated Bayern Munich to become the undisputed champions of Europe, a night in Rotterdam that lives long in the memory of the Villa Park faithful. Whilst recent success has been limited, each new season brings hope that a sleeping giant will once again rise."   A.Griffiths

ASTON PARISH CHURCH

When built in the 16th century, it was considered to be one of the finest structures in the Kingdom. The tower is 110 feet high and the spire rises a further 50 feet. It reigned over a parish of 42,000 souls in late Victorian times. The vicarage and Church Hall were demolished to make way for the Aston Expressway. In the graveyard is the burial place of Birmingham's first historian, William Hutton, 1723 - 1815.

ASTON EXPRESSWAY

The A38 (M) links the M6 with the city centre. And by staying in the right hand lane of the Expressway you can go right under the centre of Birmingham and come out the other side heading south for Longbridge. There's no central reservation. Instead the lane allocation is changed by electronic signing during the day dependent on the dominant traffic flows.

Unbelievably, the Highways Agency closed off the access to and from the M6 for 2 months in the summer of 2004 to tackle an epidemic of random potholes. The Birmingham Post estimated the cost to business in terms of hold-ups and diversions may have been £10 million on the first day alone, but the whole of the city did not grind to a halt as had been feared.

ASPHALTIC

One of 46 branches of a leading roof materials supplier that took off in Kentish Town in 1946. Everything from concrete to Welsh slate. Stock may vary from branch to branch reflecting local styles and the environment. Top frequently asked question: What is the life expectancy for felt for a flat roof? Answer: 5 to 30 years, dependent on the product used.

BIRMINGHAM & FAZELEY CANAL

In 1790 this cut from the city to Tamworth finally joined the four great rivers of Trent, Mersey, Severn and Thames into a viable national network of waterways transport with coal as the key commodity.

TRANSCO DISTRIBUTION CENTRE

National Grid Transco is the company that delivers lots of our power. The Grid do the electricity and the Transco lot look after the gas. Scary to think one private organisation has control of so much of our power supply. Transco handle 48% of Britain's energy needs and deal with over 1 million gas escape reports each year. A few days after being blamed for blackouts in the Midlands, Chief Executive Roger Urwin announced £600 million of dividends for shareholders.

HOWARD EVANS ROOFING

HQ of re-roofing specialists who are particularly proud of their refurbishment work for Forte Hotels, Iceland, Pontins, the Co-op and the University of Warwick.

NECHELLS EAST SUB STATION

Expect to see a few telecoms towers pop up here in the near future, as National Grid Transco have recently bought out the Crown Castle phone tower and TV transmission mast business for £1.1 billion in cash. So they now have a grip not just on a lot of our power but also our communication.

TDG

92,000 square feet of space devoted to storing chemicals in controlled temperatures. We were told that they are "ADR packed with full RDT functionality, primarily for the Chemical and FMCG sectors." We asked the Group Marketing Manager what all the letters stood for: ADR is German and means something like chemical operators coding; RDT is Remote Data Terminal, FMCG ("I should know this one") Fast Moving Consumer Goods.

Oh, and TDG doesn't really stand for anything, though it used to be Transport Division Group.

CLAIRE'S

Warehouse for a "specialty retailer offering value-priced costume jewelry, accessories and cosmetics mostly made in the Far East to fashion-aware tweens, teens and young adults" begun by wig manufacturer Rowland Schaefer. Apparently the lack of competition means the 650 European stores sell much more per square foot than those in the States.

5817

WASHWOOD HEATH HOLDER SITE

This Transco site has a useful Rules of Safety Notice at its entrance that begins with a poem:

"Do your bit, Play your Part, Assess the Risk before you start."

And finishes with the rules themselves:
Rule 1: Think Safe.
Rule 2: See Rule 1.

STAR CITY

Lots of girders on the outside and dark places on the inside. It proclaims to contain both the UK's largest multiplex and casino. It certainly had one of the UK's largest park and ride facilities in the summer of 2004 when the Highways Agency closed the Aston Expressway and recommended you catch a bus into Birmingham from here. On the first day of the scheme only twenty vehicles used the service. The top floor of the multi-storey was full of unsold Toyotas from the garage next door, which made it look busy. A notice warns that "Neither the Landlord or the Managers will accept any responsibility other than for Personal Injury or Death caused by negligence of the Landlord or the Managers." Stars? There are concrete hand prints on the path from the car park belonging to John Hurt and Cliff Richard.

COSTCO

You've never seen so much stuff for sale. It's one of 400 branches of an American membership cash and carry warehouse, which, if you can prove you run some sort of business, you can use for a membership fee of around £20 a year. Latest product when we visited was Item 62207: 2 pairs of Maxfli golf gloves with urethane technology reinforced leather tacky grip for improved grip in wet or dry conditions.

LDV

The home of Britain's van company, since a management buy-out, led by Allan Amey, of the troubled DAF business. Amey has built the turnover at this 85 acre site (originally home of the Wolseley Car Company), now employing 1,000 people, to £200 million. He recently got a special regional Entrepreneur of the Year award for his efforts. Biggest building visible from the motorway is this paint shop. To the west is where GEC Alstom have abandoned British train making.

IFORCE

Em, it's really hard to get your head round what goes on here. According to their website they are the UK's leading fulfilment business. What does that mean? Well, they have "created an end to end capability that enables us to offer a total outsourced fulfilment solution to our clients." This includes e-commerce and catalogue fulfilment and point of sales and marketing literature fulfilment. They have "innovative, operational... flexible, modular" solutions and can offer "very high levels of functionality" to other clients.

What do you reckon? They deliver catalogue products or something?

Murray Hennessey, CEO of John Lewis Direct declares in the sales literature that this lot are "head and shoulders above the competition."

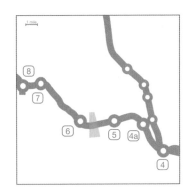

HAMPSON AEROSPACE

They make components for Rolls Royce jet engines, and supply similar French and German aircraft engine manufacturers. Hampson produce extremely finely finished shafts, combusters, casings and valves, working with exotic nickel and titanium alloys to create complex fuel system structures. Don't want those going wrong, do we!

MONTAGUE L. MEYERS

13,000 square feet of panel products and laminated flooring. One of 9 British sites of a leading timber import business. The original Mr Meyers started importing Russian softwoods at the start of the 20th century. They still bring in timber via Tilbury docks. Low point in the Editor's TV career was directing make-over shows with a couple of less than impressive blokes who enthused about veneered MDF. Doubtless such references did no harm to the Meyers sales figures.

RIVER TAME

This murky tributary of the Trent starts life in the low hills of the Black Country and makes its way eastward through some of the most industrialised parts of the country. So no surprises that it's heavily polluted.

The river contains tiny particles of metal and is the source of a considerable proportion of the copper that eventually floats into the North Sea.

BIRMINGHAM

There's the city publicity perspective, the statistics and the experience. The Editor has a rich store of memories of this place, which has provided him with most of his employment. His first big job was as a promotions scriptwriter at ATV Network, the "fun factory". He remembers the heady atmosphere prior to transmission of the "Golden Shot" on a Sunday afternoon, and of telling his Dad that he was now on nodding acquaintance in the corridors with ex-England captain Billy Wright. This was where the original "Crossroads" came from, and the Editor was party to creating what became "Tiswas" on Saturday mornings.

Next element of the Editor's working life was running a Communication Studies course at the Polytechnic. One of his most able students, Mohamed Ilyas, became News Editor of the Birmingham Post.

Then it was back to the fun factory, now trading as Central TV, to produce the daily live Children's ITV links every week-day afternoon for nearly a decade: great fun, considerable pressure and fluffy meet-the-stars territory: from Kylie Minogue to Roland Rat.

Later he had a patch at Pebble Mill, working on "The Really Useful Show" and "Call my Bluff" before they disappeared along with a host of other popular shows that the execs in London decided were no longer right for the market place. There were several thousand people working in the television industry in Birmingham 20 years ago. Now it's merely a few hundred, thanks to accountancy, market share analyses by commissioning editors and profit-taking by a few ruthless entrepreneurs.

However there is a sexy Selfridges and a golden mile of bars along Broad Street near the Convention Centre and National Indoor Arena.

Radio WM is driven by two of the nation's best anchor men, Ed Doolan and Adrian Goldberg, working in tandem on weekday mornings.

The city has over 9,000 roads, 12,000 parking spaces and 95,000 street lights.

ESSO TERMINAL

This was built in 1962 to replace a number of smaller plants across the West Midlands. It covers 30 acres and is supplied by the multi-product Midline Pipeline for white oil (petrol, diesel and heating oils), whilst bitumen comes by train from the Fawley refinery in Hampshire. 200 garages and another 200 commercial customers within a radius of about 100 miles get fuel from here.

FORT SHOPPING

Here we can find branches of many major chains including an enormous WHSmith which, when we visited, was doing a "Buy 1 Get 1 half price" on all travel writing, maps and guide books. Not a concept us small publishers much care for. In the car park is a valeting service ranging in price from £5.95 to £29.95 (off road vehicles extra). The people doing the hard work get about half the money. Top end service includes floormats cleaned and dressed, deodorising, hand polishing and bumpers gelled. This was part of the Fort Dunlop site where, back in the 1960s, a test track first identified, then solved, the scary phenomenon of aqua-planning, whereby, in very wet weather, some tyres were not touching the tarmac but just riding on a layer of water.

TYRE FORT

This enormous white building, at the northern edge of Dunlop's old site, is the 2002 British headquarters of Goodyear Dunlop, where one million tyres are stored. Dunlop Tyres were sold to Sumitomo Rubber Industries in 1984. Then in 1999, Goodyear and Sumitomo set up a "global alliance." Here they've got 47 loading bays operating 24 hours a day, preparing consignments of tyres for cars, trucks, motorcycles, agricultural and earth-moving machines all over the UK.

DUNLOP AIRCRAFT TYRES

They've been making aircraft tyres here since 1917, and currently produce 50,000 a year and retread another 25,000. Tyres for the Spitfire, Jaguar and Harrier came from here. They are currently working on the Cessna Mustang Business Jet, the Eurofighter Typhoon and the Russian Sukhoi.

MIDLAND MAIN LINE

This runs from York to Birmingham and so on to Bristol. A short way west it sits alongside what was, for more than 100 years, a big train-making plant - Washwood Heath.

Alstom announced in the autumn of 2003 that they would cease building the Virgin Pendolino tilting train here in 2004. Chances are most of the 1,900 workforce would be made redundant.

VIADUCT

Creating a motorway route that skirted around the northern edge of the City of Birmingham was a considerable challenge for Consulting Engineers Sir Owen Williams. To minimise the amount of necessary demolition, it was deliberately routed over existing canals where possible. At one stage they toyed with a two-tier structure, one carriageway above the other.

Details of the decision-making are admirably documented in George Charlesworth's formidable History of British Motorways.

More than 13 miles of this section of the M6 is elevated. Hurricane Park is a trading estate on the north side of the motorway west of here but it is accessed from a gap on the south side.

Inexplicably the carriageway towers almost directly above Tame Valley Primary School. We find it amazing that the council have never seen fit to move this school further from the fumes.

PLATFORM BUILDING MATERIALS

20,000 cash and carry products for the building trade, based on the French "La Plateforme de Batiment" model. It's part of the Saint-Gobain Group, established in France in 1665, according to their website - which conjures up an image of a man and a horse and cart collecting a few stones for the construction of a cathedral. Do they mean 1965 by any chance?

PLUMB CENTER

There are over 400 of these outlets nationally, 10 in Birmingham alone. This one has a better building than its counter area, which was small, scrappy and unmanned when we went in. We took away a quarterly Price Guide that explained that the bathroom photographs are not necessarily the "Standard Suite". Please check the details of the component parts included in the pack price before making your purchase.

BUSINESS POST

These people are attempting to snaffle a share of the Royal Mail's work. They've been at it over 30 years and now have a 7% share of the "premium express delivery market" making them the fourth largest operator in this sector.

These premises are like a fortress. You have to pass through a big metal turnstile just to reach the security office 50 metres from the building.

FORT DUNLOP

The iconic building, referred to as Base Stores, was just one of many structures on the Dunlop site that was originally occupied in 1917. When this handsome block became surplus to requirements, the Richardson Brothers, who had set up the Merry Hill shopping complex in Dudley, bought it for redevelopment. They couldn't get their plans to fruition and so it was taken over by another developer, Urban Splash of Manchester, who aim to have it operational as offices, shops and leisure facilities by 2006.

Coleman Demolition are currently removing the roof and top floor so a swanky gym can be installed for those below. Work was held up in the summer of 2004 because a pair of peregrine falcons were nesting in the rafters.

FORT DUNLOP POWER STATION

This is a highly compact affair producing 100 megawatts of electricity via a pair of Rolls-Royce industrial gas turbines. These machines are derived from the Trent aircraft engine, used to power the Boeing 777 and the Airbus A340. The gas that is used as fuel here is frequently pumped round the country underground by similar land-based Rolls-Royce gas turbines.

JAGUAR ASSEMBLY PLANT

This is where the bodyshells for the XK sports car have been made. Production has recently begun on all aluminium bodyshells for the new Jaguar XJ. And the S-type is assembled here. Previous vehicles to emerge from these buildings include, in reverse order, the Jaguar XJ6, the Mini, Morris L4 commercial vehicles, the Austin A40, A35 and A30, the Wolseley 1500, the Triumph Mayflower, the Morris Minor saloon and the Standard Vanguard.

HOLIDAY INN EXPRESS

On this site is also the Fort Jester pub (where we had a pretty good fish and chips lunch), operated by the Tom Cobleigh group, and a Wacky Warehouse. Fearlessly investigating the latter we discovered glum adults sipping soft drinks as kids went wild in baths of balls.

Amongst the Guidelines: "Party package consists of 1hr play, meal, birthday card, hats and Wack Pack. Children must be supervised at all times by their parents or another adult responsible for them. Vegetarian option does not contain meat or fish."

DURA

This American company started producing body components here for Honda, Rover, Ford and General Motors in 1991. By the mid 90s they were doing glass assemblies and trim parts, then in 2001 they commenced aluminium door production.

280 people make windscreen, rear screen and quarter light assemblies for Jaguar, door frames for Honda and complete door modules for Land Rover. The Dura Group is based in Michigan, and have manufacturing plants in North America, Brazil, Mexico, India and the Far East generating annual sales of $2.4 billion.

HODGE HILL SCHOOL

Lots of famous people visited Hodge Hill in the summer of 2004: Jack Straw, David Blunkett, Gordon Brown, John Reid. They came to the constituency, not the school, to press the flesh and kiss babies, in the desperate hope Labour could keep this by-election seat despite the distaste so many voters had for Tony Blair in the immediate aftermath of the Butler Report on the sexed up weapons of mass destruction that were never found in Iraq. Labour hung on by less than 500 votes.

The school has 1200 pupils and, thanks especially to the efforts of the cheerful and charming previous deputy head Jane Bonner, shares the site with the Braidwood School for profoundly deaf children. A £3m new block houses the deaf school and all pupils can learn sign language.

SPITFIRES AND WASHING MACHINES

The vicinity around Castle Bromwich – where lots of Jaguars are put together – has been home to machine manufacturing for a long time. In the Second World War it became a base for the production of Spitfires. After a series of delays and disputes, Sir William Morris (later Lord Nuffield) was bluntly out-manoeuvred by the determined Lord Beaverbrook when the latter became Minister of Aircraft Production in 1940. The energetic press baron handed over control of the site to Vickers, and they brought swift pressure to bear, which resulted in 10 Spitfires emerging on the freshly-created runway during June 1940. This led to an order for 500 more. But it didn't take long for the Germans to find out what was going on here and so by August it became a target for the Luftwaffe. After the first wave of destruction and death, some of the production work was dispersed to shadow factories. Winston Churchill visited in September 1941 to watch some test flights, which he described as frightening. By 1942 Castle Bromwich was regularly turning out 50 Spitfires a week. Before the war had ended the factories here had made over 11,000 of the fighter aircraft, and also produced several hundred Lancaster bombers. After the war domestic car production returned, in parallel with Bendix washing machines. The site became part of the British Leyland Motor Corporation in the 1960s.

BRITISH CAR AUCTIONS

One of 22 sites of "Europe's No1 vehicle remarketing company". Hundreds of second-hand car salesmen studying hundreds of vehicles being edged through the auction area. Goodness knows what the health implications are for the auctioneer and his colleagues, who are breathing in the fumes from every car as bids are made.

We tried to track down via the internet whether diesel or petrol fumes are more environmentally damaging. Very little sprung into sight, but eventually we came across the Co-operative Society Environmental Policy internal guidelines which suggested that diesel fumes may include particulates that could be a contributory factor in childhood asthma.

Outside British Car Auctions the traffic warden was issuing dozens of fixed penalty fines for illicit parking on double yellow lines.

SPACE 4

Here they make instant houses – well, just about. Westbury Homes have applied industrial manufacturing practices to house construction. Three shifts a day mass produce insulated and load-bearing walls and floors forming the structural panels for 6,000 4-bedroom houses a year, which is about one building per hour.

TYSELEY WASTE DISPOSAL DEPOT

What you can see is the old incinerator which is not now used, since it has become the Castle Bromwich Household Recycling Centre manned by grumpy operatives on the lookout for builders trying to smuggle in rubble.

They process around 400,000 tonnes of rubbish here each year and are dramatically improving recycling rates. More than once in waste skips staff have discovered Second World War German unexploded bombs that someone has thrown out. They treat them as live and close the site down until they have been defused.

J5

WHAT A LOT OF CARS

British car sales reached a record level in the first half of 2004, according to the Society of Motor Manufacturers and Traders. Sales averaged around 240,000 a month, which means the annual figure is over two and a half million. A third of these are diesel-powered cars. Only 18% of the vehicles sold are manufactured in the UK. In terms of manufacturers' share, Ford is still the market leader with 15%, followed by Vauxhall with 13%, Renault and Volkswagen with 7% each, Peugeot with 6% and Toyota 5%. BMW has around 4%, MG Rover just over 3% and Jaguar 1%. It all adds up to over 24 million cars on British roads.

WHAT A WASTE

One million Brummies generate half a million tonnes of municipal waste in a year. 64,000 tonnes are business waste, the rest domestic from refuse collection, street cleansing, recycling and composting activities. The City contracts out to Onyx responsibility for operating two Waste Transfer Stations and an Energy-from-Waste Plant.

Black refuse sacks are collected from 370,000 properties each week, and there are kerbside collections of paper from 328,000 households.

Each Transfer Station receives 100,000 tonnes of domestic waste, some of which goes to landfill during the day or to the Energy plant at night. There are over 400 banking sites (for paper and bottles) and five Household Recycling Centres where glass, paper, card, metals, grass, textiles, drinks cans, oil, vehicle batteries and wood are sorted for recycling or composting. 78,000 tonnes of burnt ash from the Energy plant are used in road construction.

Household rubbish recycling rates reached 14.5% in 2003, which meant a net reduction in the quantity of rubbish going to landfill for the first time. The Government's target for 2004 is 17% and for 2005 25%. There is huge variance between local authorities. Near the M6, Lichfield achieved 44%, whereas Manchester and Liverpool only recycled 2%. A third of our waste paper and plastics goes to China, without, the Guardian observes, our knowledge of the environmental or social costs.

OLD CAR MOUNTAIN

Every year over 300,000 old cars are abandoned (10,000 in Birmingham alone), each of which costs local authorities about £350 to collect and dispose of. Under new EU legislation, oil and other toxic waste from old cars has to be collected and treated to avoid contamination of land and water, which makes dismantling more expensive. The work is done by 1,500 scrap dealers, who can expect to make a small profit from the metal of each vehicle.

From the year 2007, car manufacturers will become responsible for taking back their old models, so that the last owner will be able to get rid of an unwanted car at no cost to themselves.

WARWICKSHIRE

Cars old and new in this county. It's the home of the Heritage Motor Centre, close to Junction 12 on the M40, which boasts the world's biggest collection of historic British cars, plus over half-a-million photographs in the archives. All the memorable MGs, Aston Martins, Triumphs, Land Rovers and Jaguars can be seen here.

M42

Runs east from the M5 north of Bromsgrove across to the M40 junction for Oxford, then swings north past the N.E.C. and Airport, then north east past Tamworth to Measham, where it becomes the A42 to Nottingham.

Measham was once the capital of second-hand car auctions. In the 1950s a monthly booklet detailed typical prices. You could pick up a two year old Singer 4AB Roadster for £350 (list price: £756 from the Coventry Road Works, Birmingham).

COLESHILL DEPOT

The walls of this salt barn are made of reinforced concrete lined with corrugated asbestos on wooden beams, with all fixings in stainless steel so that the building is not vulnerable to corrosion.

COLESHILL MANOR

"It is a rare occurrence when the combination of unique classical-style office suites in a landmark listed building in superb secure parkland become available. But dreams can come true and that rarity becomes reality in 2004 when the 'sleeping beauty' of the M42 awakes. Original fruit and vegetable plots have been replaced by newly-built studio-style, self-contained office suites."

RIVER BLYTHE

Runs north from Knowle to join the Tame just beyond Blyth (sic) Hall.

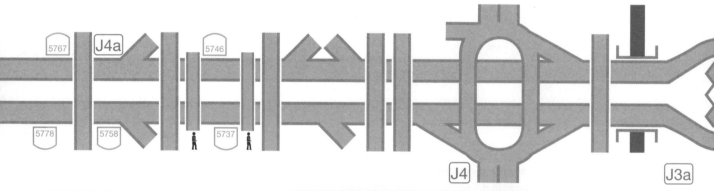

5767 J4a 5746
5778 5758 5737
J4 J3a

SELWYN HOUSE

Approaching Birmingham from the east this is the first of many tower blocks peppering some estates, here at Chelmsley Wood, then at Castle Bromwich, and then to the north past Junction 5 on Castle Vale.

Selwyn House is nearest to the carriageway, but we hope it's not typical.

In the foyer an Anti-Graffiti Hotline poster was covered in graffiti. And the House Supervisor had noted: "Certain tenants have been throwing dog mess out of their windows. This behaviour will not be tolerated and the housing department have been informed. Should I find out who is responsible then there will be appropriate action taken regarding their tenancy."

M6 TOLL

FROM HERE TOLL USERS USING OUR GUIDE SHOULD TURN TO PAGES 92 AND 93 WHERE, AFTER A FIVE MILE GAP, WE BEGIN TO INDICATE THE SIGHTS HEADING NORTHWARD UP THE PAGES.

BIRMINGHAM AIRPORT

Last year's "Future of Air Transport" White Paper confirmed Government support for BHX as the preferred site for long term airport development in the Midlands.

BBC TV news recently enthused about the airport "going global" thanks to the arrival of a new carrier, Gulf. No mention of noise or pollution issues.

Solihull

Land Rover are based here. On 1st September 2004, Ford threatened to close the plant unless it could do things better. The Birmingham Post observed: "The road map targets put forward by Ford should have made it abundantly clear that management and unions, for whatever reason in the past, had failed to talk in similar terms and their stubborn approach to various contentious issues had now reached Ford's tolerance limit. There is only one direction for both sides and that is to win a secure future for Land Rover at Solihull and no excuses." The pep talk worked!

COLESHILL PARISH CHURCH

We arrived to find this taped to the front door: "Notice of the Suspension of Presentation. WE JOHN SENTAMU by D i v i n e Permission BISHOP FOR THE DIOCESE OF BIRMING-HAM SEND GREETINGS WHEREAS the Benefice of COLESHILL and MAXSTOKE has become vacant NOW WE HEREBY DECLARE that the said vacancy shall not be filled during the period of five years from the date hereof."

RADBROOK FARM

This corrugated iron shed was where the motorway contractors tested tarmac prior to laying. It sits on the edge of this Warwickshire estate farm of 158 acres recently taken on by Philip Dyson who aims to produce 1 million litres of milk a year here from 140 cows.

CORLEY SOUTHBOUND SERVICES

Derek Stephens, a wheel-chair bound volunteer for the National Kidney Research Foundation, was sitting by the entrance when we visited. He reckoned about one in seven people passing by put a coin in his box. Just a small wooden fence separates the lawns from the motorway carriageway. Scary to view the traffic so close.

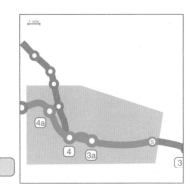

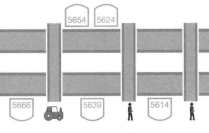

5654   5624

5666   5639   5614

SOMEONE WILL SURELY DIE

as a result of the poor configuration of feeder roads and signage where the M6, M6 Toll and M42 conjoin. There are just too many options to try to get your head round at high speed. Heading west from Corley Services is the most disconcerting approach. You may have had a glimpse of the Birmingham skyline ahead (biggest sight the BT Tower sometimes caught in sunlight in the morning, sometime a silhouette in the afternoon), then you are faced with which version of the M6 do you require, or maybe it's the M42 north, or south, or perhaps the A446? Which way is the Airport, the N.E.C., the M5? Look out for swerving, weaving and sharp braking.
It's horrible.

Coventry

Coventry makes cars, including 200,000 Peugeots at Ryton. The endeavours and industry are captured and celebrated in the Transport Museum, which claims to contain the world's biggest collection of British Road Transport. In World War Two the place made armaments and so became a constant target for the German Luftwaffe, which meant many lives were lost and buildings were destroyed.

A great history of Jaguar in Nigel Thorley's Building the Legend.

These days the road signs declare: "City of Peace and Reconciliation, Coventry inspires people." Their corporate job advertisements state: "Coventry is a city with big ambitions. We have an ambition of what we want to achieve and a multi-million pound budget to help us realise it."

TAMWORTH/LICHFIELD

See Page 93.

CORLEY NORTHBOUND SERVICES

Not often do you see untethered horses grazing on a motorway service area, but that was what we discovered on the morning of Tuesday 17th August. A group of gypsy travellers had been there overnight, after a breakdown with one of their vehicles. We pointed out to an Irishman that the horses were getting close to the feeder road coming in from the motorway. He told us the animals would see the cars coming and get out of the way.

BEDWORTH WATER TOWER

At first we tried to ignore it, taking it to be another of those supermarket instant landmarks, but it just seemed too big and so we tracked it down and were amazed at what we found. It's 40 metres high and 10 metres across, and apparently the walls are 2 metres thick. It was built in 1898 by Amos Jenkins of Southwell, Notts., for Bedworth Waterworks. It now sits in a secure compound of private houses. Quite a sight.

Nuneaton

The General Hospital opened in 1893 and issued Rules for Patients: "Visiting hours 2 to 3 p.m. on Tuesday and Friday, 2 to 4 p.m. on Sunday. Visitors shall not use improper language. They shall not give money or presents to any member of the nursing staff, nor suffer their friends to do so. If patients have any cause for complaint, they should inform the Matron." Now patients are served by the George Eliot Hospital NHS Trust.

EASCO SCRAP

This firm has four sites around the country collecting, processing and passing on scrap. We were trapped behind their weighbridge for half an hour after a couple of their skips got jammed together.

Bedworth

Veronica Moore enchanted us with her personal guided tour of the tiny museum housed in the cellar of the almshouses and put together by the Heritage Society to celebrate Nicholas Chamberlaine (1632-1715), the rector, who was a great benefactor of the place. He left a legacy to provide a good meal for every child once a year. Nowadays that just buys a bun, hence bun day in the local schools. The almshouses contrast severely with the rest of the 1960s utilitarian main street.

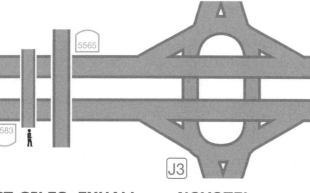

ST GILES, EXHALL

Overall winner of the 2004 Coventry Diocese best kept churchyard competition.
The bench is in loving memory of Miss Jane Masters who departed this life April 26th 1967. Her great joy was to attend the flower beds nearby. She will doubtless take comfort that her efforts have been so admirably pursued.

NOVOTEL

They've got an outdoor heated swimming pool.
Star guests: snooker players Steve Davies and Ronnie O'Sullivan, but we don't know if they went near the pool. It's one of 30 odd branches in the UK, and part of the 3,700 hotel French Accor group.

WAYSIDE BUSINESS PARK

Opened with great anticipation by a government junior minister in 1986, it's now occupied mostly by NHS Trust admin staff, apart from the west wing where we find Pro Enviro, marketing Climate Change Advantage software which allows businesses to monitor their carbon emissions.

NUNEATON-COVENTRY

Edward Churton's 1851 Rail Road Book of England's entry for Coventry points out that "No city in the empire contains more monuments of interest to the antiquarian."

JAGUAR ARENA

When it's finished – hopefully for the start of the football club's 2005 season - this will be Coventry's most impressive building at £60 million: 32,000 seats on the site of the old gas works. Jaguar are big sponsors, but anyone can contribute a brick - that will be inscribed with your own words for £39.99.

COVENTRY CRUISING CLUB

They've got moorings and a clubhouse on a short arm south off the Oxford Canal. The By-Laws include the fact that the Club accepts no liability for explosions, drownings or electrocution, or for any damage caused by fire or vandalism on the site.

Leicester

These days every two-bit tech college runs some sort of media studies course on which couch potatoes write a few essays about East Enders and make a video about their Dad's shed, and get a certificate which they anticipate will be the green light for them to direct Big Brother Series Five. Back in the 1970s the University of Leicester was a genuine and pioneering centre of excellence for Media Studies, not least thanks to the insights and diligence of the late Philip Elliott.

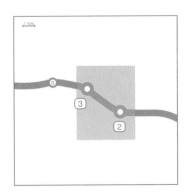

M69

Joins Coventry to Leicester, by-passing Nuneaton and Hinkley, and is one way of getting from the West Midlands on to the M1 northward.

CENTRAL MOTORWAY POLICE GROUP

170 officers use 40 vehicles (including 3 unmarked) to cover the M6 from Junction 1 to 16, plus most of the intersecting motorways, adding up to 630 carriageway miles. They deal with around 200 incidents a day, typically road traffic collisions and debris that's fallen from a vehicle. A recurrent problem is flat packs from Ikea not adequately secured to roof racks. They also have to handle all sorts of distressed animals – from dogs to elephants. In order to allow the force to concentrate more on catching criminals, some of the "housekeeping" work is being handed over to Highways Agency Traffic Officers patrolling in liveried vehicles – which causes drivers to slow down fast, thinking it's the police.

COVENTRY CANAL

Running from the Trent and Mersey Canal north of Tamworth to the Oxford Canal and hence the Thames, this was a contentious connection between the four great rivers, which Brindley had aspired to achieve. He died in 1772, eighteen years before the final segment was completed. Local lass George Eliot wrote of its "wondrous watery rings that died too soon".

JOLLY COLLIERS

This unembellished drinking hole had a core of regulars already in situ at 12.15 Friday lunchtime when we called. Between them, they couldn't think of a single thing that made the place memorable or special, but they told us they love the banter, which was jolly good.

GEORGE FISCHER

The Fischer family started making pipes in Germany over 200 years ago, and they're still at it – now worldwide. "Homopolymer polypropylene is a thermoplastic belonging to the polyolefine group and is characterised by excellent chemical and temperature resistance and has good long-term stability, the materials in fusion-jointed pipes being approved for foodstuff applications."

HILTON HOTEL

Manager Shaun's face lit up when we asked him our standard hotel question. He came up with: Jonathan Ross, Eddie Izzard, and Norman Wisdom. A standard room in August 2004 was £168. They pride themselves on their capacity to do "specialist weddings" – which means "for different cultures and nationalities".

N.E.C.

The Editor made a series of late-night factual programmes for ITV, half of which were shot here. "Gaz Top Non Stop" required Gareth "Gaz Top" Jones (from "How2" and sundry other kids' shows) to walk and talk his way round exhibitions, meeting exhibitors on the way and finding out what they were there to show. And it was unedited; instead a continuous recording, each part typically 17 minutes, the cameraman, Robin MacDonald walking backwards down the aisles between the stands, adjusting focus, framing and iris on the hoof. It's the biggest exhibition centre in Europe with 4 million annual visitors.

MOBBS WOOD FARM
David Power enthusiastically farms 300 acres. Summer 2004 was the worst for weather for nearly 20 years, much of his corn having been flattened and soaked. He'll dry it (with expensive diesel) and use it for animal feed. His beef cattle go to a slaughter house in Guildford at the age of 26 months in order to become Marks and Spencer beef. They looked very content grazing in a field that is criss-crossed with the remnants of a medieval village.

Lutterworth
Locals vividly remember the day in 1963 when the M1 opened and suddenly this place became a quiet town, no longer accomodating all traffic between Rugby and Leicester.

Coombe Abbey
They run a medieval banquet evening here that the Editor attended many years ago whilst researching for his dinner-theatre project, Spaghetti Junction, in which actors mingled anonymously with guests until their characters burst into song or battled with spouses and secret lovers, leading ultimately to the hurling of cake and pasta across the venue. Not everyone's cup of tea.

OXFORD CANAL
77 miles worth, joining the Coventry Canal to the River Thames. Engineered by James Brindley, it started to deliver coal from the Midlands to Oxford in 1790, replacing shipments from Newcastle-on-Tyne brought down the North Sea and up the Thames.

NUNEATON-RUGBY
This is the West Coast Mainline. It was along here on 20th September 2004 that a Virgin Pendolino (she that tilts) set a new speed record for London to Manchester of 1 hour 53 minutes.
The track improvements that allowed this achievement cost £7.6 bn.

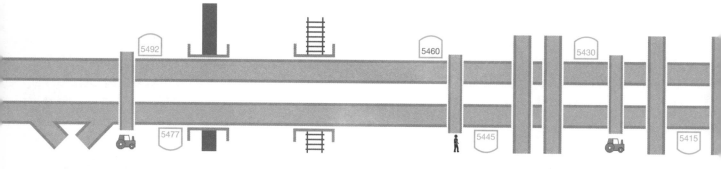

CATHEDRAL
"Awesome, moving, spectacular and uplifting" are comments in the Visitors Book. "The New Cathedral rises above the Ruins of Old St. Michael's as a testament to the strength of forgiveness and reconciliation, and a symbol of hope in a world still in conflict." The original cathedral church was demolished by Henry VIII. A millennium project allowed archeologists to explore the ruins which are now platformed in the Priory Visitor Centre.

ROLLS ROYCE, ANSTY
This is where they maintain gas turbine engines for helicopters, fighter aircraft and passenger jets. The site was developed by Armstrong Siddeley in 1935 to train pilots for their Avro Cadet aircraft. The Standard Motor Company assembled Airspeed Oxford and de Havilland Mosquito aircraft here. After the war it was used for top secret rocket testing.

Warwick
The University's Automotive Centre is endeavouring to "deliver Applied Research and Technology Transfer into the Premium Automobile Sector", including a web-based shop floor information system to reduce the "transmission time of business critical transactions specifically utilising Lean Production Methodologies... to resolve quality issues with suppliers".

Hinkley
There is a sobering trio of time-shift photographs of the town in John Stretton's nostalgic look at Leicestershire since 1945. The contemporary scene of functionality and traffic management have replaced 1950s street stalls, a coach-built pram, a Morris 8, an Austin 7 Ruby and a helmetless motorcyclist.

HOLY TRINITY, CHURCHOVER

Mary Short and Doreen Bradbury have compiled the definitive volume on this village. Two of the pews in the church were permanently reserved for King Edward VII and his party, who were frequent visitors to nearby Coton House, now occupied by the Royal Mail (the house, not the pews).

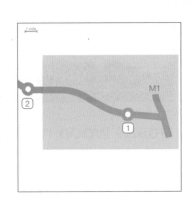

1 mile

Leicestershire

In the second edition of their Leicestershire and Rutland guide of 1924, Messrs Harvey and Crowther-Beynon declare: "We are now in a position to say something of the scenery. Though it has neither mountain, sea, nor lake, and makes no pretension to rival what may be called the show counties, it has a placid but quite individual beauty, and certainly does not merit the description flat and ugly, by which it is usually dismissed by those who have not visited it intimately."

Felixstowe

The newly created A14 skirts from the end of the M6 east past Kettering, Huntingdon, Cambridge, Bury St Edmunds and Ipswich to reach the largest container port in the UK handling almost half of Britain's deep sea container trade.

M1

We aim to discover the joys of this route in our next book. Any suggestions for content gratefully received. Write to us at severnpix, P.O. Box 468, Worcester WR6 5ZR.

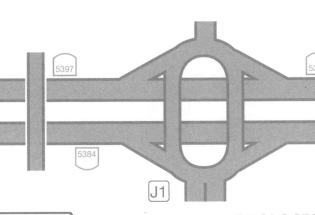

5397 5363

5384 5350

J1

Rugby

School Head Goulburn documented its history in 1856: "And forwards still it went; ever answering the good intent of our religious founder and rearing many a profitable member of the church and commonwealth, until one came to rule it who from that place sent a new vital power thrilling through every school in England: Arnold." Where is it? Head for the giant cement works.

PROLOGIS/ PEARSON/GAP INC.

Giant sheds, low profiles. The first (heading west) is another achievement by Prologis in impacting on the landscape. The middle one is full of Penguin books, and in the summer of 2004, they wouldn't come out. A massive publishing cock-up meant that the automated system to stack and track books didn't work and so lots of new titles were lost inside despite having got great reviews in the press. Next shed along is full of clothes belonging to Gap, who, worldwide, shift close on $4 billion's worth per quarter.

CATTHORPE

You can just glimpse the crowning glory of Catthorpe Manor Farm's shop clock-tower.

This was a model farm dating from 1882. It's now a mixed farm of 700 acres. The shop sells Matthew Grindal's strawberries in the summer and his Mum's cakes in the winter. She has a Fortnum and Mason award for them.

RADIO MASTS

On the horizon in August 2004 we could see the last remaining Very Low Frequency radio masts that provided communication to British submarines at sea. Most were demolished in June 2004.

HISTORY

A journey down the M6 takes us along the oldest section of motorway in Britain, and the most recent. We traverse the Preston by-pass, and, 110 miles further south, we have the option of exploring the M6 Toll.

Both these segments of the carriageway were developed in an atmosphere of controversy, not to say bitterness. Millions of us have benefited from the perseverance of the planners, negotiators, financiers and contractors, but people living in the vicinity or, worse still, along the path of those stretches (the first a mere 8 miles, the second 27 miles), suffered greatly for our subsequent travelling convenience.

1896 was the year in which motor cars were first legally permitted to use the roads. Through the first half of the 20th century British road-building schemes had been initiated piecemeal and politically to relieve unemployment rather than to reduce congestion or road accidents. There was no grand strategy or continuity of approach by the Ministry of Transport, which was strongly lobbied by powerful railway interests. In 1938 there were 4,450 miles of trunk road, of which only 27 miles were dual carriageway, whilst elsewhere in Europe and in the USA sophisticated systems of dedicated trunk routes were substantially driving the economies and providing easy access to distant parts.

In 1945 the Ministry of War Transport issued a paper proposing principles for new post-war Special Roads in the UK, on the basis that existing roads could never be satisfactorily adapted to accommodate the anticipated future levels of motor vehicle use.

Major H.E. Aldington, Chief Engineer, declared that it would be necessary to have "dual carriageways for up and down traffic, the elimination of vehicular traffic cuts at road intersections, the elimination of the crossing of vehicular, pedestrian and cycle traffic on the same level, the elimination of standing traffic, the gradual feeding-in of one traffic stream to another at points where two flows join, a simple system of

direction and warning signs, a uniform running surface, the provision of lay-bys every few miles to permit vehicles to stand off the carriageway, and strict limitation of frontage access." This was a military plan that more or less came out right. What we eventually got was that which the good Major had recommended, apart from the lay-bys and access to frontages. Thank goodness those elements were shot down.

Half-a-dozen new by-passes were proposed in the Trunk Roads Act of 1946, which also initiated a comprehensive survey of future road needs for the country. The 1949 Special Roads Act triggered the commencement of Lancashire's Bamber Bridge- Broughton new road around Preston and the county's Hampson Green- Carnforth scheme. Work commenced on the Preston by-pass in 1956. It opened in December 1958 as the first length of motorway available for public use in Britain. The survey for a proposed motorway between Preston and Birmingham was almost complete by this time. So commenced a decade of intensive motorway construction.

Harold Watkinson, Minister of Transport and Civil Aviation, declared in 1957: "Our duty lies in deeds not words. If we can have less verbiage and more mileage of road construction completed we shall be making a real contribution to the cause of better roads in fact and not in projection or plan." He kick-started the creation of 400 miles of dedicated carriageway. By 1970 there were 660 miles of motorway in Britain, which meant that, since the Preston by-pass opened, the average rate of expansion of the motorway system had been about one mile each week; and this rate then increased so that there were over 1,400 miles by 1980.

Junction by junction, for those anoraks amongst us, on the M6 this breaks down chronologically as follows: the Lancaster by-pass opened in April 1960; the Stafford by-pass in 1962; the Thelwall bridge to Preston section in July 1963; and the Stafford by-pass to Thelwall in November 1963. Lancaster

to the M55 (J32) opened in 1965; Junctions 10 -13 opened in 1966; the Penrith by-pass took effect from 1968; 1970 saw Carnforth joined to Penrith and the creation of the Carlisle by-pass, and in 1971 Carlisle was joined to Penrith. Finally in 1972 Sir Owen Williams's designs for the route from the M1 to Bescot came to fruition.

The success of the civil engineering means we are utterly unaware of it. The carriageway passes effortlessly through valleys and along hills, across rivers, railways and canals as well as other roads. We sweep on and off feeder roads on to other carriageways with almost no sense of the design and engineering that has gone into the construction of a thoroughfare that sturdily and safely traverses problematic terrain and integrates with or sits comfortably alongside other transport routes.

Across the West Midlands much of the M6 has been built on huge stilts above roads and canals. Through Cumbria enormously complicated engineering efforts were required to cut carriageway space out of hillsides, and to fill valleys and lakes with the extracted rock to provide a base for embankments and bridges.

Clever men and hard-working men did all this. A few of the workers died in the process; many lived a joyous cowboy lifestyle for some years, which they still remember fondly.

The disruption for those who lived close to the route was huge, and some have never come to terms with the change.

'Compulsory purchase' has a draconian ring and individuals and families have been scarred by its application. Through his massive estates in Cumbria the Earl of Lonsdale personally took on the task of designing and negotiating the route past his tenants, and apparently satisfied many parties and saved the Department of Transport lots of money by his decisions.

These days supermarkets seem to be the critical power-brokers. They argue they are simply meeting our needs and pepper their planning applications with gestures of contributing to the community and creating jobs. But essentially the firms employ "Property Managers" whose function is to swamp any counter arguments to supermarkets extending their tentacles across the landscape.

As indicated in the Introduction, I came to see the drive up the M6 as more than a passage past premises and, instead, as a journey through our contemporary culture. The 24-hour temples of trolley shopping that sit on the outskirts of Carlisle, on the promenade at Whitehaven (and which so many of us enthusiastically support) are eliminating the variety of our communities, the nature of our jobs and adding to the quantity of traffic on our roads. Many farmers we spoke to told us a bitter story of how they had been treated by supermarket buyers – often trained and deployed to never develop an empathetic relationship with their suppliers. I sat in many a transport café surrounded by glum drivers taking a lonely break from conveying another vast load of provisions from one part of the country to another.

Working through the M6 Sights Guide you acquire a sense of what our country has become, and I for one don't think it's enriched by many of the mass-produced, identical goods and our seemingly insatiable appetite for more. The charms of the texture of a town like Penrith are in constant danger of dying; elsewhere, in places like Bedworth, they are desperately close to extinction.

Recording the history and sights of the M6 has included opportunities for the Editor to recall his own associations with the artery, particularly between Birmingham and Manchester. At points along the carriageway he was reminded of incidents and emotions, mostly related to his working life in Birmingham and visits to his parents' home in Manchester.

Nowadays there are well over 100,000 vehicles on the M6 on a typical day, twice as many south of the M62 Manchester-Liverpool intersection as to the north of this vital junction.

Stephen Bayley, reviewing histories of motoring, observed that we have made a deadly Faustian transaction: mobility in exchange for death and despoliation. There are 28 million vehicles on British roads. More than two and a half million new cars were sold last year, the highest figure for 13 years. But 3,000 people died in road accidents; that's around 10 a day.

The motorways are the setting for 1,600 people being killed or seriously injured each year. Recently that included someone committing suicide by walking on to the M5. Worst motorway crash to date took place on the M6 near Forton Services in 1985 when a coach and ten other vehlcles collided, some bursting into flames. This left 13 dead and many others injured.

But the motorways are our safest roads in terms of injury per mile travelled, a handy Department of Transport measure of these things.

And Britain is one of the safest countries in which to travel by car. Worldwide 1.2 million people are killed or seriously injured in road accidents each year.

As for the lorries: Felicity Lawrence estimates that four out of every ten lorries we pass are transporting supermarket products between depots and outlets. The typical lorry costs £90,000, weighs 38 tonnes and is driven 100,000 miles a year. The transport of food by lorries and in shopping trips by car causes 3.5 per cent of the total carbon dioxide emissions into the atmosphere in the UK.

Only one in seven of us regularly uses public transport.

YES, WE LOVE OUR CARS.

Can there be environmental or economic inhibitions to the level of use of our vehicles? Will the decline of availability of oil and its rising price lessen our annual mileage? Are we persuaded to pay for a faster route between two points? The jury is out as the take-up figures for the M6 Toll indicate.

Can the motor industry come up with effective alternatives to oil before that fossil fuel dries up?

Every journey along the M6 costs us more, and churns out more pollutant that dirties the air and contributes to global warming, with immeasurable repercussions for the long-term health of the planet.

And yet M6 motoring allows us to visit the Lake District whenever we feel like it, to have kiwi fruit every day of the year, to visit sickly relatives at a moment's notice.

It is hard to imagine circumstances in which fewer vehicles would one day be using the road.

You will encounter the evidence and advocacy of environmentalists along our route. We trust such observations will enrich your understanding of the world we inhabit and so ready traverse.

BIBLIOGRAPHY

We have been fast, and frequently shallow, readers of booklets, brochures, gravestones, leaflets, maps, menus, newspapers, notice-boards, pamphlets, posters, signs and (almost always as a last resort) websites.

(And nothing matches turning up, taking a look around, knocking on a door and asking what goes on here.)

Ordnance Survey maps and Streetmap print-outs have proved vital in comprehending the geography that we have then ruthlessly distorted to fill the spaces on our pages.

Many of the texts to which we have referred are mentioned within the relevant entry, but the essential books that have given us a bigger picture are as follows:

TRANSPORT IN BRITAIN	Philip Bagwell and Peter Lyth
A HISTORY OF BRITISH MOTORWAYS	George Charlesworth
BRITISH CANALS	Charles Hadfield
MANCHESTER SHIP CANAL	Ted Gray
NOT ON THE LABEL	Felicity Lawrence
SHOPPED	Joanna Blythman
CAPTIVE STATE	George Monbiot
HOW WE CAN SAVE THE PLANET	Mayer Hillman
THE YELLOW EARL	Douglas Sutherland
THE LINOLEUM MAN	Philip Gooderson
TALES OF OLD RAILWAYMEN	Tom Quinn
GREAT RAILWAY BATTLES	Geoffrey Body

Diggy, who has been a big help, guarding the Editor's N-reg Rover 214, with 140,000 on the clock and still going strong.

Whilst there was plenty of coal-mining in these parts, it was never very strongly unionised, according to A.J. Taylor's history of the Staffordshire Coal Industry. The Cannock Chase Miners', Engineers' and Surfacemen's Association was first formed in 1887, many years after other unions. By 1892, only half of the county's 44,000 miners were unionised.

LODGE FARM

This has been where Walkmyll Great Danes have been bred for the last 40 odd years. Freda Lewis has created 30 champions and is a senior judge and was secretary of the Great Dane Society. Husband Ron started planting trees 10 years ago to protect the property from the noise of the Toll road and, even worse, from the new by-pass that lies between the motorway and his house.

LAKESIDE PLAZA

HQ of Electrium, an electronics company handling everything from micro components to switchgear. The developer told us that land prices have risen four-fold since the arrival of the M6 Toll and he's now working on putting up a big hotel near junction T4.

M6 NORTH

IF YOU ARE FOLLOWING OUR SIGHTS NORTHWARD, THEN FROM HERE YOU JUMP TO PAGES 62 AND 63 WHERE THE TOLL IS REJOINED BY THE MAIN CARRIAGEWAY.

1489   1478

1498   T8   1487

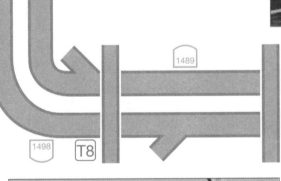

HIGHWAY ROBBERY

Reginald Thomas used to live where you are now travelling. Compulsory purchase meant he was offered a sum of money for his land and compensation to build a new house and farm buildings to the south. He considered the figure far too small based on the price of similar properties in the area. He was given a proportion of the sum offered and has personally built a new bungalow and farm outbuildings, and is struggling to achieve a satisfactory settlement through a land agent.

T.J. EDWARDS

Occupying the big mustard and brown buildings is a firm that conveys car body shells across Britain and Europe. Most of the shells are made in Europe and brought into the UK, eight to a lorry load. They have been here since 1987, and despite the arrival of the M6 Toll at their doorstep, they don't use it because of the cost.

Between here and Mr Thomas's building is a maintenance shed. MEL run their own support services for the toll road.

IBSTOCK

They make piles of bricks here, and have won a host of Brick Development Association awards for their work. Colours are currently big: gloss green, blue, white, yellow or burgundy; or satin honey, lemon, pink, sky blue and sage.

For capped garden walls they recommend an ingenious invisible locking system that creates a very heavy monolithic mass which lasts well and resists displacement by weather or vandals.

UNILEVER WAREHOUSE
It's 31 metres high and provides 45,000 square metres of floor space for packets of soap powder, tubs of margarine, and all the other stuff that will be decanted to various supermarkets around the Midlands. It's on Kingswood Lakeside, a new development initiated by Cannock Council on an old open cast coal mine.

NORTON CANES SERVICES
The lady topping up the CDs and audio cassettes told us they don't sell much smutty stuff here, due to the limited number of lorries using the toll road. In fact, the site has a certain up-market feel in her opinion and she's going to try some business skills cassettes on the shelves. To the west is the chimney of Norton Aluminium Products, a secondary smelter recycling car bodies. The steel cone on top propels fumes higher and faster from the furnace discharge point.

AUTOMOTIVE LIGHTING
The big silver shed made car lamps until recently. Now the work is transferring to cheaper factories in central Europe. One of the security guards asked us for a job.

STAFFORD-WALSALL
This now under-used commuter line used to be the freight connection route from the Cannock coalfields to the West Midlands conurbation.

SAINSBURYS
In 2003 they got a ticking off from the Independent Television Commission for a Jamie Oliver commercial that claimed "only Sainsbury's sell a range of tempting twenty-one day beef". Consumers and butchers complained that most independent butchers sell such meat. (See Joanna Blythman's "Shopped – the Shocking Power of British Supermarkets").

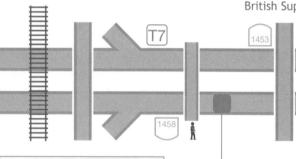

FACOM
This is a headquarters of a big French-owned tool production company. They do Sykes-Pickavant diagnostic machines, Britool industrial instruments and Facom automotive equipment. The products are mostly made overseas and distributed from here. Biggest sellers: manual torque wrenches and electronic code readers for deciphering data from your car engine's circuitry.

GT WYRLEY TOLL PAVILION
On the 13th August 2004, after 8 months, Midland Expressway Limited gave a prize to their 10 millionth customer, Adrian Wells of Cannock, who commutes to Burton every day. In the early days the Toll Road was accused of deliberately pricing lorries off its route to save on maintenance costs. After six months they shifted prices slightly against cars and in favour of lorries.

TURF LODGE
You can just spot the top of this big M&B eatery and drinkery, where we saw this sign: "During the summer months we are currently experiencing excessive amounts of flies due to the surrounding countryside and wasteland. We are with many other pubs and businesses in the area that are experiencing these problems. We welcome any suggestions to eliminate the problem and during your visit we apologise for any inconvenience this may cause."

CHASEWATER

Breaking our own rules we want to tell you about the view over the embankment to your north. It's like a visit to the seaside. 300 hectares of water in a reservoir created to service the Midlands canal network. There's even a crazy golf course. In the foreground is the Forest of Mercia Innovation Centre.

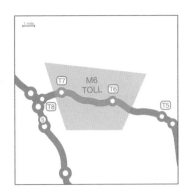

RAILWAY SHEDS

These new buildings house old rolling stock, some of which can take you on a trip round Chasewater at the weekends on the last bit of the Cannock Chase coalfield rail network.

WHARF LANE SCRAP

Andy Taff has been operating motor recycling and skip hire from here for many years. There'll be radical changes soon when new legislation on the recycling of cars comes into effect. Instead of "smash and bash" they'll spend lots of man-hours separating out the oil, petrol, trim and tyres – which means it'll cost us more to get rid of our old cars.

LICHFIELD AQUEDUCT

You know that Inspector Poirot with the greasy little black moustache – yes, David Suchet's version? Well, the actor's a big canal buff, and he put his weight behind a campaign to persuade the toll road builders to stick in a structure that could carry the Lichfield - Hatherton Canal across the motorway at some time in the future, if the Trust can raise the money to pay for its reinstatement around here. All parties consider this nominal bridge a great achievement, but we find it hard to imagine how funds will ever be found to erect sets of locks on either side of the structure to get the water and boats across.

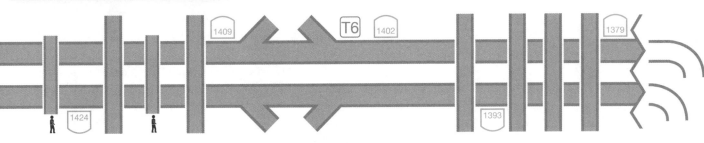

1409 T6 1402 1379

1424 1393

Rugeley

We know this place best for the Raptor Rescue Centre, a small charity run by a dedicated wildlife enthusiast, Mick Cunningham, who takes in injured hawks and falcons, often after they have been found at the side of the road having been hit by a motor vehicle, and he tends them until they are able to fly again.

CASTINGS

They are ductile and malleable iron founders, able to provide raw, coated or finished machine parts up to 25 kilos. By increasing the Silicon and Molybdenum content of spheroidal graphite iron, its heat resistance and strength at high temperature is increased, which has a valuable application in car exhaust and turbo charger systems.

TRAVELLING TOWARDS COVENTRY, THE TOLL ROAD GRADUALLY TURNS SOUTH HERE.

WE'VE GOT A 3 MILE GAP, AFTER WHICH, AT THE TOP OF PAGES 90 AND 91, WE SHOW THE TOLL ROAD GOING DOWNWARD.

Brownhills

19 events made up the Memorial Hall entertainment Programme for 2004, including a Skittles Night with Fish and Chips, Kate's Party Fun and Sing-a-long for the over 50s, and Disco 60s: theme: 'Schooldays' St. Trinian look-alikes welcome. Other activities: Brownhills Towns Womens Guild, Pound Shredders, Karate Classes for Children, Aldridge Music Comedy Society and Blood Transfusion Service. All events bring your own drinks.

Burntwood

In 1902 the Lichfield Mercury published Chronicles of Cannock Chase, which explained: "Burntwood, a hamlet in the parish of Hammerwich, palpably discloses the origin of its naming as traceable to a forest fire. A Forest jury of the year 1262 formally recorded that 'a certain heath was burnt by the vills of Hammerwich to the injury of the King's game'".

SHENSTONE HALL FARM

Chris Abel was shocked when he first saw the plans for the Toll road in the village hall, because the route lay right across this big new shed. Apparently the planners hadn't walked the course and were unaware of it. So they moved the motorway 50 yards east to accommodate the buildings rather than pay the compensation to relocate them. Chris decided to diversify and started providing plant hire for the motorway construction – tractors and water tankers. And he's now getting similar work on new road builds in other parts of the country.

SHENSTONE CHURCH

The Reverend Richard Bailey is lucky to have Shenstone, and Shenstone is lucky to have him. He tries to meet the spiritual needs of everyone in the pretty village. About 100 people come to a service each Sunday. The sandstone tower of the old church still stands next door. English Heritage expect it to be maintained, but that's a huge demand on the church's coffers.

Richard points out that the Parish Church is not a monument, but a place where visitors are always welcome.

SUTTON MAST

This provides a big chunk of the West Midlands with their TV signals. What a difference a good press officer can make. NTL across the road were swift and effective in responding to our requests for information on their sites, whereas Crown Castle who operate this place ignored our calls for weeks on end.

Sutton Coldfield

This was a run-of-the-mill cluster of feudal dwellings until John Vesey was born in the middle of the 15th century. He turned out to be a high flyer and got in with the Royals, which led to his appointment as Bishop of Exeter in 1519. He also did a bit of private tuition around the Palaces, not least for Princess Mary, daughter of Henry VIII. And on the strength of this the King saw fit to grant Vesey's home patch a charter for self-government in 1528. This meant they could call the place a Royal Town. Oooooooo.

THICKBROOM BARNS

The black barns belong to another victim of the chosen line of the motorway. When we met the farm owner he was patently finding it very difficult to come to terms with the inconvenience of how his land has been reduced and altered to accommodate the carriageway.

WEEFORD QUARRY

Believe it or not this Hanson sand and gravel plant had nothing to do with the construction of the motorway, which mostly lies on natural sand and gravel. The works have been here since the 1940s under various ownerships, digging down 15 metres to provide 20 tonne loads to concrete businesses in a 30-mile radius. And there's plenty more where that came from.

WEEFORD PARK FARM

A couple of hundred free range pigs can usually be seen on 30 acres here.

Each sow spends one week with a boar. 3 months, 3 weeks and 3 days later she gives birth to a dozen or more piglets each weighing half a kilo. They leave their mother after 4 weeks, and after 13 weeks (when they have reached 35 kilos) go to another farm for another 10 weeks to take them to 90 kilos, at which point they will be slaughtered. Farm manager Anita Blakemore is a vegetarian and does her very best to give the animals a happy life here.

MIDLAND EXPRESSWAY CONTROL

Operational HQ for the toll business lies north of the east-bound feeder road off the carriageway at Junction T4. The civil engineering cost £485 million and was carried out by Cambba, a construction group consortium of Carillon, Alfred McAlpline, Balfour Beatty and Amec, that built 34 new bridges along here. Midland Expressway hold the concession to operate the motorway for 53 years.

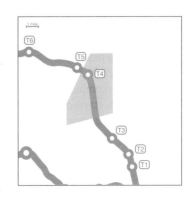

BLACKBROOK ANTIQUE VILLAGE

What was an old farmhouse and yard has been turned into a cornucopia of period delights. It's full of salvaged farm, house and church fittings, artefacts and bits of architecture. You can check out the highlights of the ever-evolving stock at www.blackbrook.co.uk.

WEEFORD PARK

Who said no-one is using the Expressway? This was at six on a Thursday afternoon nine months after it opened. Average daily figure for usage of the system in the summer of 2004 was 55,000. Most of the toll booth attendants are female, which some newspapers observed is sexist and others see as sexy.

Burton

In 1744 William Worthington set up a brewery on the High Street, and so founded the town's worldwide reputation for beer. William Bass became a near neighbour and by the 20th century there were few pubs in England that did not have some bottles on the shelves that had come from here. What fine work the good people from these parts have done.

PROTEST

The Northern Relief Road (as this thoroughfare was originally known) did not appear without a fight, most of which took place just south of here, where some cottages were destined to be demolished. Alongside the campaigning endeavours of the Not in My Backyard burghers of Sutton, many green activists undertook courageous. determined, and occasionally life-threatening action to frustrate the planners and engineers moving forward. People chained themselves to trees, dug tunnels into the line of the carriageway and locked themselves down there. The building affected 100 sites of ecological interest.

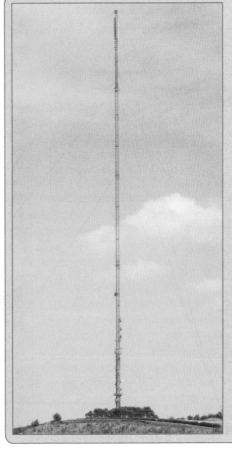

LICHFIELD MAST

NTL provide Channel Five, and FM and Digital radio services from this 1,000 feet high structure. Nationally, NTL transmit ITV, Channel 4 and Five signals to around 22 million UK homes (i.e. almost all of them). They've got 2,300 radio sites across the UK, and they also operate a Public Safety division providing communication support for police, fire and ambulance services.

IN DENIAL

"The UK leads the world in rhetoric on climate change, but while the Government remains in denial about the growing contribution of road traffic and flying to climate change, this is just hot air. The Government is doing little more than biting its finger nails on transport and the environment and failing to do anything significant for fear of upsetting motorists," say Transport 2000. They want the Government to publicly make the connection between growing traffic and use of planes and environmental disaster in the long term.

INTERMEDIATE TOLL PAVILION

These aren't always manned (or womanned) as we discovered one Saturday morning. If you don't have the right change (the machines don't take notes) or a credit card, what do you do? Buzz them and beg them to let you through? Or reverse back up on to the main road? We recommend the former. By the way, the tariffs are a bit less if you're not doing the full 27 miles.

Kingsbury

For a comprehensive pond-by-pond guide we suggest you visit www.fisheries.co.uk/kingsbury. Or go and have a look at the 15 sparkling pools across 600 acres.

MOXHULL HALL HOTEL (N.O.)

Travelling north you can see the old water tower above the Annexe. The hotel itself is to the west, and was hosting a wedding reception when we arrived. We walked into Reception and were offered a glass of champagne by a smart-looking waiter, but he was not smart enough to click that we were patently not dressed for a posh do."

RYE FARM

Over 1,000 acres are devoted to potatoes, wheat, oil seed rape and barley. The new shed is to store potatoes, which the Watts family supply to 50 greengrocers across the Midlands – washed and pre-packed in all popular sizes from 4 bakers-in-a-tray to 25 kilos in a bag.

CEMBRE (S.O.)

British HQ of an Italian firm (pronounced "chembray") who make and distribute electrical connector and installation equipment.

DENT WIZARD (S.O.)

For £85 plus VAT they can remove a dent the size of a tennis ball from a panel on your car as long as the paint isn't damaged.

BIRMINGHAM-FAZELEY CANAL

Walk along the towpath eastward and you'll soon come to the Heart of England Way trail. Keep going and you'll reach Drayton Manor Park, but you can't get in without paying.

RIVER TAME

It's just come past a huge acreage of sewage works, so despite anything the Environment Agency might tell you, don't get too close.

BEAVER METALS

They acquire non-ferrous metals from all over the world – things like taps, sinks and copper boilers – break them down and sell them on – again to various parts of the world. They are interested in factory clearances and will pay cash. Copper is the most valuable end commodity; so much so that the premises are surrounded by an electrified fence in front of which is a moat.

Coleshill

In the Domesday book it is noted that "There are 30 villeins with a priest and 13 bordars with 16 ploughs." It became the seat of the Digby family, who were given Coleshill in 1495 by Henry Tudor for supporting the Lancastrians in the Wars of the Roses. The Manor dates from 1871 (see page78). The Wingfield-Digbys cleared off in the 1920s. And guess what the place now has on its High Street. Yes, a sweet little Tesco, of course.

BIRMINGHAM -TAMWORTH

This is the main line from the West Midlands to Derby and beyond.

T3

1202

1191

T1

1170

LANGLEY MILL MASTS

The little bunch of big masts down the hill from the Archers' depot belong to NTL. It's the medium wave site for independent local radio in Birmingham.

ARCHERS

The family have been delivering fork lift trucks all over the country since 1972. And we are very pleased to hereby document that if they get any new business as a result of the exposure in this Guide, the boss, Paul, told us, in front of two witnesses, that he would pay us 5% of the value of that fresh work. So if you've got a fork lift truck that needs moving get in touch with these charming, helpful, efficient, good-looking people, and mention our name.

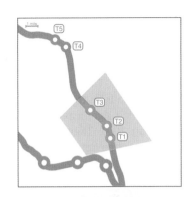

The Belfry

The Editor was given a personal guided tour of the course by its top pro. Not for this book but as research for a 15 part digital TV series he made called "Tim Brooke-Taylor's Golf Clubs". Yes, the old Goodie is a fair golfer, and many a happy day was spent on various courses where Tim played against the resident pro. Not an easy thing to shoot on a single camera compared to the ten on crane arms that the BBC have for their coverage.

Drayton Manor Park

100 attractions in 250 acres of parkland. The Pandemonium - turns your world upside down. Maelstrom, the awesome gyro swing - beyond the limit. Apocalypse - "Britain's scariest ride" ("The Sunday Times"). Eh, like, they're experts?

FREEMAN MILK DEPOT
(S.O.)

Four generations of Freemans have been shifting milk. They started as Birmingham milkmen and now work for the Midlands Co-op, collecting in 27,000-litre articulated tankers from 120 farms across Warwickshire, Derbyshire and Leicestershire. They came here to Dunston Wharf in 1986, and suffered little disruption during the construction of the Expressway.

Lichfield

What's a hitherto peripatetic bishop? One that wanders around a lot, having no fixed place of worship. Kettle and Johnson's History of Lichfield Cathedral leaves no stone unturned in detailing the developments. For instance, St. Chad, Bishop of the Mercians, stopped being peripatetic and took a seat here from 669 to 672. Then after his death his bones were put in a wooden shrine and became a popular object of pilgrimage. These days we find here headquarters of a large, successful, mutually-owned organisation with strong links to the community and a proud record of adopting ethical and socially responsible policies benefiting members and the wider public - the Midlands Co-operative Society.

Tamworth

This place has a huge building full of skiers heading down slopes of snow. It's an enormous indoor skiing centre that must cost a fortune to run. As global warming continues it may eventually become a centre of pilgrimage for those who want to remember what snow looked like.

CONCENTRATE

We have not featured any sights south of here because we reckon it requires every ounce of concentration from everyone in the vehicle to successfully negotiate the next few miles where the M42 runs in parallel with the Toll road and you can read the signs for both, though only one lot are relevant. The orange boxes are built into the concrete separating shoulder. It's not good.

THE MAIN CARRIAGEWAY JOINS UP 5 MILES FURTHER SOUTH-EAST, ON OUR PAGE 78.

INDEX

INDEX